mum's favourite recipes

mum's favourite recipes

classic home dishes from mothers of leading chefs and other friends

compiled by Bill Tikos

LANTERN

an imprint of
PENGUIN BOOKS

Contents

Introduction vi

Breakfasts and brunches 3

Soups, starters and light meals 17

Pasta and rice 47

Main courses 71

Desserts, cakes and biscuits 139

Acknowledgements 172

Index 173

Introduction

My many memories of growing up in Melbourne in the seventies and eighties are dominated by the image of my mother busy cooking in the kitchen. In our house, the kitchen was more than just a place to prepare food: it was the epicentre of family life. For Greeks, food is as much about bringing people together as it is about nourishing the body. For Mum, food and cooking are a celebration of life and an expression of her love for her family and friends. She always cooked extra (and still does) in case one of my countless uncles, aunties or cousins dropped in. And drop in they did – particularly when they heard she was making her legendary baklava.

This book pays tribute not only to my mother but to many other mums too. Alla Wolf Tasker recalls summer afternoons in Daylesford where family friends came to share her Russian mother's wonderful delicacies. Guy Grossi remembers with great affection the comforting calamari pasta his mother would serve every Easter. Dorinda Hafner says her mum's west African pink risotto was served at just about every special occasion and became like another member of the family . . . The list is endless.

Of course, star chefs and celebrities are not the only ones who have been inspired by their mums' cooking. Tucked away in most kitchens there's a well-worn exercise book filled with recipes — hand-written, cut from magazines and newspapers — passed down from grandmother to mother to daughter (or son), a treasure trove of culinary secrets. But secrets they are no longer, thanks to the generosity of this book's contributors in sharing their much-loved family recipes.

Mum's the word no more.

Breakfasts
and
brunches

Sunday-morning crêpes

Fiona Hoskin

Sundays in our house were special family times. My mum, Ellen Pitts, cooked a special breakfast for us – delicate, thin crêpes sprinkled with sugar and eaten with a squeeze of fresh lemon juice. We crowded around the stove as she cooked them, eating them as they came out of the pan! If she was lucky she got to eat some after we had all had our fill. I still cook them sometimes and fondly remember those carefree, happy days.

Makes about 16 crêpes

1½ cups milk
¾ cup plain flour
1 tablespoon castor sugar
2 eggs
1 teaspoon vegetable oil
pinch of salt
zest and juice of 3 lemons
¼ cup castor sugar extra, for serving

Place half the milk in a mixing bowl with the flour, castor sugar, egg, oil and a pinch of salt, and beat until smooth and creamy. Add the rest of the milk and whisk to combine. Strain into a jug and leave to stand in the fridge for 30 minutes.

Add the lemon zest to the crêpe batter. Cook very thin crêpes in an oiled pan until lightly golden on each side. (They will be very fragile, so take care when turning them, but persevere as they are moist and luscious!) As each crêpe is cooked, sprinkle with castor sugar to taste and squeeze lemon juice over, also to taste. Roll up, and eat immediately.

Fiona Hoskin was born in New Zealand, the eldest daughter of British parents who had emigrated from Britain. She has lived in Tasmania for twenty years and her restaurant Fee and Me, which opened in 1989, has scooped numerous awards including 'Best Restaurant in Australia' in the American Express Awards in 2000.

Riz au lait (sweet rice)

Meyjitte Boughenout

This was a regular Sunday breakfast prepared by my grandmother, Mila Velimanovic. She is Yugoslavian, but this is not completely a traditional dish – it is one she created while living in France. When I was away at cooking school I would come home every weekend and I always looked forward to Sunday morning. The problem was keeping me away from the fridge on a Saturday night, after she had put the rice in to set.

I remember that my grandmother would spend all day every day in the kitchen preparing and cooking food. I think this is where I found my desire to be a chef and to experiment with food.

Serves 4

2 litres milk
100 g sugar
140 g rice
1 vanilla pod
60 g butter
4 egg yolks

Bring the milk and sugar to the boil, add the rice and vanilla pod, return to the boil and then turn heat down and simmer for about 20 minutes. Remove from heat, then add the egg yolks and butter, and whisk for 1 minute. Pour into small cup moulds and leave overnight in fridge to set.

The following morning, unmould the rice on individual plates and serve with chopped fresh seasonal fruit.

Meyjitte Boughenout worked under some of France's leading chefs before, at twenty-five, receiving his first appointment as an executive chef. Crossing the world to become executive chef in the Dining Room Restaurant at Sydney's Ritz-Carlton, he soon won accolades for his light, modern style. He later moved to Tasmania to become executive chef and co-owner of the boutique hotel Franklin Manor, since awarded three hats by the *Guide to the Wine & Food of Tasmania*.

Rakott burgonya (layered potato bake)

Iren Kurek

I learnt to cook from my mother, who is now ninety and still enjoys cooking. In my experience, this dish has been a success with everyone who tried it, regardless of nationality. Back in Hungary we used to have it as part of the main meal, following the inevitable soup. However, it could equally well be served for brunch, as an entrée, or just as a snack.

It's best to buy the type of potato that doesn't crumble when it is boiled. I have found Desiree to be a good choice.

Serves 4

1 kg medium-sized potatoes

6 eggs

100 g streaky bacon, unsliced

200 g ham off the bone *or* smoked pork sausage

2 cups sour cream

1 tablespoon butter

2 tablespoons dried breadcrumbs

salt

grated cheese for topping (optional)

Wash the potatoes carefully and boil them in their skins in salted water until cooked. Drain in a colander and let cool.

While the potatoes are cooking, prepare the other ingredients. Hard-boil five of the eggs. Dice the bacon finely and fry until most of the fat has melted. Drain off the fat. Cut the ham into 5 mm squares, or, if using sausage, slice into coins. Spoon the sour cream into a jar, break in the remaining egg and beat lightly with a fork for a few seconds.

Coat the bottom of a casserole dish with the butter and then sprinkle the breadcrumbs on top.

When the potatoes have cooled, peel and slice them into 5 mm thick rounds. Shell the boiled eggs and slice with an egg slicer.

Preheat the oven to 180°C.

To assemble, place one layer of the potato rounds on the bottom of the prepared casserole dish and sprinkle with a little salt. Follow with one layer of eggs, then with a layer of ham and fried bacon pieces or sliced sausage. Spoon over a third of the sour cream mixture.

Repeat until you run out of ingredients, reserving enough potatoes for the top layer. (Otherwise, cover the top with breadcrumbs.) Sprinkle grated cheese over the top, if desired, and bake, uncovered, for 30 minutes. Watch that the cheese doesn't burn.

Serve with a choice of salad.

Iren Kurek arrived in Australia from Hungary in 1957 and married an Englishman. She self-published a cookbook entitled *Lifting the Lid off the Goulash – Things My Mother Taught Me*, and currently lives in Adelaide.

Village eggs

John Bedelis

Visiting my grandmother, Koula Kefalas, was always a culinary delight. All the wonderful times I spent with her remain with me through her traditional home recipes, which I still cook almost every day.

Village eggs reminded Grandma of when she was a young girl living in the northern part of Greece in a small village. Early in the morning she would run out to collect the freshly laid eggs from the barn for breakfast, while her mother would prepare the wood-fired oven to bake the daily bread. Now village eggs remind me of her.

Serves 4

6 large free-range eggs

2 tablespoons extra-virgin olive oil

50 g Greek fetta cheese, crumbled

1 handful fresh herbs (try basil, oregano and flat-leaf parsley), roughly chopped

home-made bread, thickly cut and toasted

salt and cracked black pepper

Crack the eggs into a bowl and gently break the yolks, being careful not to mix the yolks and whites together. Heat half the oil in a large non-stick frying pan over low–medium heat. Pour the eggs into the pan, then add crumbled fetta and most of the fresh herbs on top. With a spatula, slowly and gently slide through the mixture several times in different directions. This allows the mixture to cook through slowly, creating a light, rippled, layered effect.

Serve immediately on toasted bread, drizzle lightly with the remaining olive oil, season with salt and cracked black pepper then garnish with the remaining herbs.

Draughtsman John Bedelis developed a passion for good food and traditional Greek cooking at a young age, thanks to the delicious food he encountered at convivial family gatherings. Today he proudly keeps alive these delightful memories through his own family, wife Amanda and son Jett, and enjoys nothing more than creating good food accompanied by fine wine for great friends – the recipe of Life.

Steamed savoury pumpkin cake

Anthony Lui

The oven was not popular in Hong Kong when I was young; most of the Chinese mums did not know how to bake cakes forty years ago. The majority of the snacks we had were either steamed or pan-fried. This steamed pumpkin cake is liked by everyone in the family, as the sweetness of the pumpkin makes it so different. It can be served hot as soon as it is made, or it can be placed in the fridge then cut into slices and pan-fried whenever we feel like having it.

Makes about 16 pieces

6 medium-sized dried Chinese mushrooms

3 tablespoons oil

3 shallots, peeled and chopped

3 lap cheong (Chinese pork) sausages, finely chopped

150 g green prawn meat, finely chopped

1.8 kg whole pumpkin

3 teaspoons salt

⅓ teaspoon pepper

360 g rice flour

125 g plain flour

1 spring onion, thinly sliced

1 stalk parsley, finely chopped

Soak the mushrooms in ¼ cup of water for 1–2 hours. Squeeze out excess water, then remove and discard the stalks. Cut mushrooms into small pieces.

Heat the oil in a wok over low–medium heat, add the shallots and fry until golden brown. Pour the shallots and most of the oil into a container for later use, leaving behind 1 teaspoon of oil in the wok. Add the sausage, prawn meat and mushroom and stir-fry for 1 minute over medium heat.

Remove the skin from the pumpkin and cut the flesh into chunks. Boil over medium heat until soft (approximately 20 minutes). Drain and mash. Add the sausage, prawn and mushroom mixture, the shallots in their oil, and season with salt and pepper.

Mix the two flours together and gradually add to the pumpkin mixture, stirring until it thickens and becomes smooth. Pour mixture into a greased pan and steam for 90 minutes over high heat. Test with a skewer. If no mixture sticks to the skewer then it is ready. Otherwise, steam for another 20–30 minutes.

Remove the pumpkin cake from the pan. Cut into the sizes that you want, sprinkle with spring onion and parsley and serve immediately.

Originally from Hong Kong, Anthony Lui has worked as head chef at the Flower Drum, in Melbourne, since 1981. The Flower Drum, which many consider to be Australia's best Chinese restaurant, has won the American Express Restaurant Awards consistently since 1988, and been awarded the title of Restaurant of the Year three times by the *Age Good Food Guide*.

Corn fritters with fried eggs and bacon

Jared Ingersoll

This dish, courtesy my mum Angela Ingersoll, is the best breakfast in the world! The fritters are easy to make, tasty, and versatile: they're great as a snack or as a canapé, and can be served with whatever your imagination suggests – though in my family there is only one thing to do with a corn fritter, and that's eat it with eggs and bacon. *And* only serve this dish on a cold morning, when the family is all there. Believe me, I have tried in vain to cook it for dinner, for lunch and for a midnight snack, for just myself and with friends, but it somehow doesn't taste the same. The batter can be made the night before, which will give you another twenty minutes in bed!

Serves 4–6

1 tablespoon butter
1 onion, finely diced
6 cobs of corn, kernels removed
400 ml cream
2 eggs
about ½ cup flour (you may need more if the corn is too wet)
salt and pepper
eggs and bacon as required

Melt the butter in a saucepan and cook the onions until soft (2–3 minutes). Add the corn kernels and cook for a further 5 minutes. Then add the cream and cook for another 5 minutes or so, until the cream is slightly thickened. (Mum would use the mixture at this point to make the fritters, or if she wanted to be fancy she would blend the corn until it was a coarse purée.) Allow the mixture to cool before adding the eggs and flour. Season to taste with salt and pepper.

In the morning, go straight to the kitchen, turn the oven on full and leave its door open to warm the kitchen. You will need 2 nice big frying pans: divide the bacon between both pans, so as to leave a nice bit of bacon fat for cooking the eggs and fritters. When the bacon is cooked, drain it on paper towels and place in the oven to keep warm while you open all the bedroom doors (the aroma will be enough to get everyone out of bed and to the table on time). Spoon the corn batter into one pan (each fritter should be about the size of a pikelet). When they are starting to set and colour, flip over to cook the other side. It is now that you should start to fry your eggs.

When everything is just about cooked, take the whole lot – pans and all – to the table, so everyone can serve themselves. Serve with a big pot of tea, toast, and tomato sauce.

Jared Ingersoll worked in London at Mezzo, The Square (two Michelin stars) and Hillaire before becoming head chef at the Bayswater Brasserie in Sydney. He opened Danks Street Depot in 2002, and six months later it won Best Café in the *Sydney Morning Herald* Good Food Awards.

Soups,
starters
and light
meals

Cullen skink (smoked cod, salmon, scallop and potato soup)

Michael Wood

This is a recipe that my grandmother (my father's mother, Frances Wood) used to make for me in Scotland. Every Friday, from the age of six until I was around twelve years old, I would go to my grandmother's, and during winter she would always make *Cullen skink*. The dish originated in the picturesque fishing village of Cullen on the Banffshire coast. *Skink* is an old Scottish word for 'broth'. The original dish uses smoked haddock, which is unavailable in Australia. This is my version of my grandmother's secret recipe.

Serves 6

400–450 g smoked cod fillets

300 g butter

750 ml milk

2 large onions, peeled and finely chopped

4 large Nicola (or other waxy) potatoes, peeled and cut into 4 mm dice

2 litres fish stock

1 cup chopped curly parsley leaves

200 g smoked salmon, finely diced

2 fresh bay leaves

salt and pepper

cream (optional)

18 large Queensland scallops, roe removed

grapeseed oil

chervil sprigs, to garnish

Select a flameproof casserole dish that is just large enough to hold the cod in a single layer. Grease the dish lightly with some of the butter and lay the cod on the base. Pour the milk over. Place the dish over medium heat on the stovetop and gently bring to simmering point. The liquid should be just shimmering, not boiling. Allow cod to poach until tender (about 8 minutes). Carefully lift the cod from the dish, reserving the milk. Place the cod on a chopping board and, when cool enough to handle, remove and discard skin and bones. Flake the flesh into a bowl and refrigerate for later use.

In a large saucepan, melt the remaining butter over medium heat. Add the onion and cook until soft and transparent. Add the potato and continue cooking for 5 minutes. Add stock, parsley, smoked salmon, bay leaves and enough salt and pepper to season. Simmer until the potato is tender, then strain in the milk retained from cooking the cod. Add the flaked cod. Check and adjust seasoning if required. Add cream, if desired. The soup will be quite thick. Keep warm over very low heat.

When ready to serve the soup, use a small, sharp knife to lightly score the scallops in a cross-hatched pattern on one side only. Heat a small, heavy-based frying pan over very high heat. Brush scallops lightly with oil and quickly sear, first on the scored side then turning after about 30 seconds. Scallops are best served rare.

Ladle soup into bowls and place 3 scallops, cut-side up, in each bowl. Garnish with chervil sprigs and serve immediately.

Michael Wood was born and bred in Edinburgh. He started his apprenticeship there at the renowned Prestonfield Hotel in 1974, and came to Australia to live in 1985. He has been executive chef at Brisbane's Pier Nine since 1994 and has played an integral role in the restaurant's garnering of many industry awards, achieving the highest rating of three stars from *Australian Gourmet Traveller* over four successive years from 2001.

Cock-a-leekie soup

Judy Davie

Serves 6

1 large chicken

1 brown onion, chopped

2 sticks celery, chopped

1 tablespoon olive oil

2 carrots, grated

6 leeks, washed and shredded

¼ cup long-grain rice, rinsed in cold water

salt and pepper

1 tablespoon chopped parsley

This soup my mum, Biddy Davie, used to make is so comforting on a cold winter's day – and in Scotland there were lots of those. Sometimes I use brown rice, though my mum never did.

Make a chicken stock by bringing the chicken to a boil in a large saucepan with 2 litres water, the onion and the celery. Cover the pan and simmer gently for 1½ hours. Allow to cool, then skim off all fat before straining the stock. Remove the nicest chicken meat from the carcass, slice and set aside.

Heat the olive oil in a large saucepan and add the carrot and leek. Sauté for about 4 minutes, then add the chicken stock, chicken meat and rice. Bring to the boil then simmer, covered, for 45 minutes. Season to taste with salt and pepper and add parsley just before serving.

Judy Davie coaches people to enjoy the benefits of eating healthier food. Her interest in macrobiotic cooking and food as medicine led to her involvement in the popular television show *Search for a Supermodel* before she founded her company, The Food Coach. She writes a column for *Woman's Day* and features regularly on ABC Radio. Her cookbook *The Food Coach* was published in 2004.

Split pea and ham soup

Jill Dupleix

When I grew up, there always seemed to be a great big pot of pea and ham soup on the wood-burning Aga in winter. It was there at the end of the walk home from the school bus, and it was there after my brother Tony and I had been tadpoling in the dam, sliding on the frost-covered lawn or creating homes out of hay bales, ready to warm frozen fingers and provide a bit of central heating. Mum (Rosemary Dupleix, or Ro as she was known) does a great pea and ham soup, and every winter I continue the tradition, serving it as a meal with a slice of grilled sourdough bread on the side. The carrots, celery and onion add freshness, the smoked ham imbues a lovely sweetness, and the split peas contribute that wonderful pea-soup texture that brings it all together.

Serves 6–8

1 kg smoked ham hocks

500 g yellow split peas

4 carrots, peeled and chopped

4 sticks celery, chopped

3 onions, peeled and chopped

2 bay leaves

sea salt and pepper

2 tablespoons roughly chopped flat-leaf parsley

Place the ham hocks, split peas, carrot, celery, onion and bay leaves in a stockpot, cover with 3 litres water and bring to the boil, skimming off any froth as it rises to the surface. Simmer gently for 2 hours, partly covered, skimming if necessary.

Remove the ham hocks and shred the meat, discarding bone, skin and fat. Whiz half the pea soup in a blender and return to the pan with the shredded ham. Taste for salt and pepper (some ham can be quite salty), gently reheat and then serve scattered with the parsley.

Jill Dupleix is one of the most influential Australian food writers. The author of eleven cookbooks, Jill now lives in London, where she writes and photographs her weekly food column for the *Times Weekend*. Her recipes and writing also appear in *BBC Good Food Magazine*, *Food and Travel*, the ABC magazine *delicious*, and *Australian Gourmet Traveller*.

Grandma Hewitson's borscht

Iain Hewitson

Our mothers and grandmothers had little choice but to follow the principle that if the produce wasn't in the garden or on special at the local market, then it rarely made it onto the table. My Scottish gran Annie Hewitson certainly understood this philosophy. Bringing up a large family (composed predominantly of coal miners), what that woman couldn't do with a pile of bacon bones, a whole lamb's liver or, when it was close to payday, whatever could be gleaned from the garden had to be seen to be believed. This soup became a family favourite which, for want of a better name, I've called a borscht, mainly because it always included beetroot – a vegetable that thrived in New Zealand's glacial Edinburgh of the South, Dunedin.

Serves 6–8

4 medium–large beetroots, peeled and chopped

¼ Savoy cabbage, chopped

1 onion, chopped

2 sticks celery, chopped

1 medium-sized carrot, peeled and chopped

1 parsnip, peeled and chopped

2 tablespoons chopped parsley

a good splash of red-wine vinegar

¾ cup tomato purée

1–2 cloves garlic, crushed

water or vegetable stock

salt and pepper

6–8 baby potatoes, peeled and halved

½ cup sour cream

1 tablespoon horseradish cream

1 tablespoon chopped fresh chives

Place beetroot, cabbage, onion, celery, carrot, parsnip, parsley, vinegar, tomato purée, garlic in a large stockpot, and add water or stock to cover. Put the lid on the pot, bring to the boil and cook for 20–25 minutes, or until the vegies are tender. Blend the soup and check seasoning.

While soup is cooking, boil potatoes in plenty of water until tender.

Mix together sour cream, horseradish cream and chives. Set aside.

To serve, put 2 potato halves in each bowl, pour in soup and place a dollop of the sour cream mixture on top.

New Zealand-born Iain Hewitson has been a chef/restaurateur for more than thirty years. He has owned many restaurants in Melbourne, including, for the past fourteen years, Tolarno Bar and Bistro. He has also fronted a number of television shows, and currently appears on *Huey's Cooking Adventures* on Network Ten. He has written five books and issued a range of sauces, the most popular being his Kick Arse BBQ Sauce.

Ajiaco (soup of leftover barbecued ribs)

Angel Fernandez

This is a version of the delicious traditional soup/stew *ajiaco*, which is very popular in Chilean households. At home, Dad would be in charge of the barbecue (*asado*) on days of celebrations or parties. Kilos and kilos of meaty and succulent ribs, together with garlicky South American chorizos and blood puddings, would go on the rustic and gigantic coal-powered grill. People would gather around the barbecue and nibble furiously as the meat came off the grill, washing it down with a rich *vino tinto*. The next day Mum would carefully slice the meat from any leftover barbecued ribs and make it into this hearty and flavoursome soup.

Serves 4

2 medium-sized onions

3 tablespoons olive oil

300 g barbecued rib meat (pork or beef), sliced into long strips

4 cloves garlic, finely chopped

1 teaspoon sweet paprika

1 sprig oregano

1 litre chicken stock

4 large pink-eye (or other waxy) potatoes, cut into wedges

1 large carrot, sliced

1 bay leaf

salt and pepper

4 eggs

2 tablespoons roughly chopped flat-leaf parsley

Cut each onion into 4 wedges without cutting all the way through to the root end.

Heat the oil in a deep saucepan and fry meat until well browned. Add garlic and cook without colouring, then add paprika, oregano and stock. Bring to the boil, then simmer for 10 minutes, skimming constantly.

Add potato, carrot, bay leaf and salt and pepper, and continue cooking until the vegetables are almost cooked. Add onion and simmer for a further 4 minutes. Check seasoning again, then add the eggs and poach for 2 minutes, throw the parsley in and serve carefully, trying not to break the eggs.

Chilean-born Angel Fernandez migrated to Australia with his family in 1986. After training in this country to be a chef, he took a job at Rockpool with Neil Perry, where he worked for five years before joining Catalina Restaurant in 1995, where he is now executive chef.

Warm chicken soup

Michele Cranston

My grandmother, Margaret Mackenzie (we called her Granny Mac), was a wonderful woman who, unusually for her time, had lived a full life acting, travelling and teaching before she settled down to married life. As such she was quite an elderly grandparent, and my memories of her are as an old woman complete with walking stick and aches and pains. That didn't hold her back in her enjoyment of friends, good books and life, however.

She was not a great cook but her few favourite dishes she did exceptionally well. I remember a wonderful chicken casserole that was always made when you were ill, large jars filled with short-bread biscuits swirled with jam, small jars holding the sugary delight of home-made barley sugar, and her afternoon-tea pikelets served with lemon juice, butter and a sprinkle of sugar. But it was her soup which became a family staple. Whenever we'd visit for lunch, the menu would always be the same. There were no complaints from us; it wouldn't be lunch at Gran's without her yummy, fresh-flavoured soup served in pretty flowery bowls, plates of buttery toast and an extra bowl of grated cheddar cheese for scattering over the steamy soup. As a child you'd watch the cheese slowly sink into the soupy vegetables before you plunged your spoon into the warming broth.

Serves 4

2 tablespoons olive oil
2 rashers bacon, finely chopped
2 white onions, finely diced
1 carrot, peeled and grated
1 bay leaf
1 turnip, peeled and grated
2 large potatoes, peeled and diced
2 sticks celery, thinly sliced
2 single chicken breasts, finely diced
1.5 litres chicken stock
sea salt and white pepper
½ cup roughly chopped
flat-leaf parsley

Heat the oil in a large saucepan and add the bacon and onion. Sauté over medium heat until the bacon has browned, then add the carrot, bay leaf, turnip, potato and celery. Stir for 1 minute, then add the diced chicken and chicken stock. Bring almost to the boil before reducing the heat to simmer for 30 minutes. Season according to taste with salt and white pepper and add parsley just prior to serving.

For a richer version you can garnish with a tablespoon of sour cream or some grated cheddar cheese.

Michele Cranston has been the food editor of *marie claire* (Australia) for four years and has written four cookbooks in the *marie claire* series. Working as a chef for seventeen years in various kitchens, she recalls as the highlights setting up the kitchen of bills in Sydney with Bill Granger and running the kitchen for a busy production company in London.

Chicken liver pâté

Anna Last

My mother, Mary Last, has been my greatest culinary inspiration. Her gift for flavour and her appreciation of simplicity and good ingredients are the basis of my approach to cooking. Mum's pâté made an appearance at any family gathering while we were growing up – picnics in the paddock or dinner parties – and we never got tired of it. It is still the best I have ever tasted.

Serves 6–8 as an entrée,
or 16 as an appetiser

500 g chicken livers, trimmed
½ cup brandy, port *or* sherry
100 g butter
1 onion, peeled and chopped
fresh thyme leaves
½ cup cream
salt and pepper
2 teaspoons lemon juice

Place the chicken livers in a bowl and cover with the brandy. Cover and refrigerate for at least 2 hours, or preferably overnight. Drain the livers and reserve the liquid.

Heat a frying pan with half the butter and sauté the onion and a teaspoon of the thyme leaves. Add the drained livers and cook, in batches, until browned on the outside but still pink in the centre. Transfer to a food processor. Then, working quickly, pour the reserved brandy into the frying pan and stir to pick up all the brown bits. Add the remaining butter and the cream and bring to boil to reduce the liquid a little. Season to taste with salt, pepper and the lemon juice.

Blend livers, gradually adding the reduced cream from the pan. Blend until very, very smooth. Push through a sieve to make the pâté extra smooth. Spoon into ramekins or pâté dishes and refrigerate for at least 24 hours before serving. If keeping for any longer than a day or two, cover with clarified butter and it will last for a week.

Anna Last began her cooking career standing on a chair in her mother's kitchen, 'helping' to make meringues. She is the food editor with *Vogue Entertaining + Travel* and writes, cooks, and produces menus for and styles the pages of the magazine.

Russian trio

Alla Wolf Tasker

My mother, Katherine Wolf (or 'Baba'), was a fabulous cook. Our Daylesford summer house was surrounded by a prolific orchard and vegetable garden, and the back verandah was always covered with stoneware urns filled with dilled cucumbers and tomatoes, and salted cabbage. On weekends, many Russian friends arrived bearing contributions to what was essentially an endless table of the small delicacies Russians call *zakuski*. These were enjoyed with shots of vodka and were composed of salads, cured fish (including home-smoked eels), tongue and hams with freshly grated horseradish from the garden. My favourites from my mother's *zakuska* table included what I call my 'Russian trio', and I am delighted to share these recipes with you.

Serves 6

Jellied eel and smoked trout
600 ml clear fish stock

3 saffron threads

4½ gelatine leaves

salt and white pepper

300 g boned smoked eel fillet

300 g boned smoked trout fillet

25 g cooked green peas

Stuffed eggs with horseradish
6 hardboiled eggs, shelled

100 ml good-quality mayonnaise

20 g strong horseradish cream
(freshly grated horseradish is best)

salt and white pepper

Russian salad
180 g cooked beetroot, cut into
½ cm dice

180 g cooked potato, cut into
½ cm dice

100 g dill cucumber, cut into
½ cm dice

mustard dressing

For the jellied eel and smoked trout, heat the fish stock in a saucepan, add the saffron threads and allow to infuse. Meanwhile, soak the gelatine leaves in cold water until soft. Drain and squeeze to remove excess water. Add to the hot fish stock and stir until dissolved. Taste and adjust seasoning with salt and white pepper.

Cut the smoked eel into batons and the smoked trout into dice. Divide eel, trout and peas amongst 6 moulds (I use sections of PVC pipe with plastic film attached to the bottom). Top with the fish stock and refrigerate until set.

For the stuffed eggs, slice a little egg white off the bottom of each hardboiled egg so they will stand upright. Then slice off just enough white from the top of each egg to gain access to the yolk, and scoop out yolk with a teaspoon. Mash the yolk with the mayonnaise and horseradish until smooth. Adjust seasoning with salt and white pepper, then place the mixture in a piping bag. Fill egg whites with the mixture. Refrigerate until ready to use.

For the Russian salad, toss beetroot, potato and dill cucumber with mustard dressing until well combined. Refrigerate until ready to use.

To assemble the Russian trio, place a stuffed egg on 6 individual plates. Unmould the jellied eel and smoked trout (you may need to place the moulds in a little warm water to do this) and place one on each plate. Position a piece of 4 cm diameter PVC pipe on a plate and fill with Russian salad, pushing down with a spoon. Lift off the PVC piping and repeat for the other plates.

Alla Wolf Tasker is executive chef of Lake House in the central Victorian town of Daylesford. The award-winning restaurant is known for its sophisticated seasonal and regional cuisine. In 2003 Alla was honoured with the title 'Living Legend' by the Melbourne Food and Wine Festival and received the *Age*'s Professional Excellence Award for her commitment to excellence and the mentoring of young people in the industry.

Chilli prawn, asparagus and avocado cocktail

Christine Manfield

Serves 4

2 tablespoons olive oil

2 cloves garlic, minced

4 drops Tabasco sauce

½ teaspoon chilli paste

16 green king prawns

zest and juice of 1 lemon

½ teaspoon coriander seeds, roasted and ground

sea salt and white pepper

1 tablespoon shredded coriander leaves

Cocktail sauce

4 tablespoons mayonnaise

3 tablespoons tomato sauce

1 teaspoon Worcestershire sauce

4 drops Tabasco sauce

1 tablespoon lemon juice

2 teaspoons grated horseradish

sea salt and freshly ground black pepper

Salad

6 asparagus spears

½ avocado, sliced

8 cherry tomatoes, quartered

2 spring onions, thinly sliced

4 iceberg lettuce leaves

4 sprigs coriander

One taste treat produced by my mother Fay Manfield, which stands out in my memory from youthful days, was the classic symbol of style of that time – the prawn cocktail – served simply with shredded iceberg lettuce. For us it was always a ceremonial offering, served up on birthdays and the like, rather than an everyday event, and as kids we always loved it. Queensland summers and prawns somehow always seemed to go so naturally together, and all this dish required of Mum's time was the quick shelling of spanking-fresh prawns and the whipping up of a quick cocktail sauce.

The prawn cocktail has seen something of a revival in more recent times, and here I have adapted the original idea from Mum by cooking the prawns with a dash of heat and adding avocado and asparagus to the salad, as these basic ingredients are so accessible these days and make for a more luxurious offering. For me it remains a summer favourite and a treat.

Heat the oil in a frying pan with the garlic, Tabasco sauce and chilli paste.

Shell and de-vein the prawns and halve them lengthways. Add to the frying pan and sauté gently for 2 minutes, or until prawns begin to change colour. Add lemon zest and juice, and the ground coriander, and season to taste with salt and pepper. Remove from the heat and add coriander leaves. Allow to cool.

To make the cocktail sauce, whisk all sauce ingredients together in a bowl until combined. Taste and adjust seasoning to suit.

For the salad, slice the asparagus spears thinly on the diagonal and then blanch. Mix the cooked prawns with the asparagus, avocado, tomato and spring onion in a bowl. Set each lettuce leaf onto a serving plate and add a spoonful of the cocktail sauce. Arrange the prawn salad on top, then spoon over some extra cocktail sauce.

Garnish with a coriander sprig and serve immediately.

Christine Manfield established an international reputation with Paramount Restaurant, Sydney, which she opened in 1993 with partner Margie Harris. She recently opened East@West, in London's Soho, which was awarded Tatler's Best New Restaurant for 2004 just four months after opening. Christine has written four successful cookbooks.

Halwa sabji (vegetable halva)

Hemant Gusain

My mother, Shivi Devi Gusain, introduced me to the power of the pumpkin at an early age when I received the flower of the pumpkin, mildly spiced and fried, as my first solid food. Ma used every part of the pumpkin – the leaves, the seeds, the vegetable and the flower – in some way or another. Mealtimes were always well attended, and Ma always included pumpkin on the menu, either as a savoury or a sweet dish.

This special wedding-party dish of halwa sabji (the chief ingredient of which is, of course, pumpkin) is one of my favourites.

Serves 4

2 tablespoons vegetable oil
1 teaspoon mustard seeds
5 dried red chillies
2 cloves garlic, finely chopped
2 onions, finely chopped
2 tomatoes, finely chopped
½–1 teaspoon salt
1 teaspoon chilli powder
1 teaspoon ground coriander
1 teaspoon ground turmeric
1 kg peeled and cubed pumpkin
½ cup water
sprigs of coriander, to garnish

Heat the oil in a large, heavy-based frying pan, add the mustard seeds, dried chillies and garlic and cook over medium heat until the ingredients start to crackle. Add the onion and sauté for a few minutes, then add the tomato, salt, chilli powder, ground coriander and turmeric and stir well. Cook for a minute or so, then add the pumpkin and water, mix well and cover with a lid. Reduce the heat to low and simmer for 30 minutes, stirring occasionally.

To serve, garnish with fresh coriander and eat either as it is or with rice, bread or plain yoghurt.

Indian-born Hemant Gusain began his cooking career at Claridge's Hotel, New Delhi, before moving to the prestigious Hotel Taj Mahal. After travelling to Switzerland on a one-month work placement to promote the Indian Food Festival at the Hotel Du Rhone, he came to Australia, where he eventually established Siemer's Indian Restaurant in the Adelaide Hills.

Stuffed green capsicums and tomatoes

George Bilionis

Whenever there was a special occasion, whether it was Christmas, Greek Easter or even somebody's birthday, my family would make the trip to the home of my grandmother, Victoria Bilionis, for a feast fit for a king. As well as lamb on the spit, slow-roasted potatoes, beautiful braises and of course her world-famous fried rice, Grandma would serve up stuffed tomatoes and capsicums. As soon as the oven opened, the aromas that filled the room would mesmerise us.

Serves 4

4 large, firm tomatoes

1 teaspoon sugar

4 large green capsicums

¾ cup long-grain rice

4 tablespoons olive oil

1 onion, chopped

¼ bunch flat-leaf parsley, finely chopped

500 g tomatoes, peeled and chopped

2 tablespoons tomato paste

salt and freshly ground black pepper

6 mint leaves, finely chopped

½ cup dry red wine

500 g minced beef *or* lamb

2 cloves garlic, crushed

Preheat oven to 180°C.

Cut a thin 'lid' off the top of each tomato. With a teaspoon, scoop out the pulp, chop it and set it aside for the stuffing. Sprinkle the inside of the tomatoes with the sugar, then place them upside down to drain.

Cut the top off each capsicum, scoop out and discard the seeds. Plunge the capsicums and their lids into boiling water and simmer for 3 minutes. Drain, then refresh in cold water.

In ½ cup of water, parboil the rice.

Select a heavy-based frying pan and put over low heat. In 2 tablespoons of the oil, sauté the onion until it is soft and transparent, then add the parsley. Add the reserved tomato pulp, the peeled and chopped tomatoes, and the tomato paste, salt and pepper, mint and wine. Mix well and simmer over low heat for 20 minutes, stirring occasionally. If the mixtures dries out, add some water.

Separately, in the remaining oil, fry the meat until brown, stirring constantly. To the meat add the parboiled rice and two-thirds of the tomato sauce. Cook this stuffing over low heat for 10 minutes, stirring occasionally. If necessary, add some water to keep the mixture moist. Remove from heat and cool.

Stand the capsicums and the tomatoes in two separate baking dishes and, with a teaspoon, fill each loosely with some stuffing. Replace the lids, pour the remaining tomato sauce into the dishes and cover with foil. Put the capsicums into the oven first, then 20 minutes later put in the tomatoes. Continue cooking for another 15 minutes, then remove the foil from both dishes and cook for a further 10 minutes, removing the lids so you can baste the stuffing mix. Serve hot with the remaining tomato sauce.

George Bilionis started his career on the Greek island of Ithaca, where he fell in love with Greek culture and food. When back in Australia, he hooked up with Cath Claringbold to further his professional career, and through her fell in love with Middle Eastern cooking. In 2004 he opened his first restaurant, Souk, in Melbourne.

Moussaka

Simon Johnson

This is one of my favourite recipes, as it reminds me of my mother's cooking: good, honest home food. Mum, Maureen Johnson, grows all her own vegetables and herbs, and believes that straight out of the garden is best.

Serves 4

2 eggplants
2 tablespoons olive oil
500 g minced beef
2 onions, chopped
2–3 cloves garlic, minced
1 × 400 g can peeled tomatoes
1 teaspoon dried oregano *or* a handful of fresh oregano
1 teaspoon sea salt
black pepper

Cheese sauce
2–3 tablespoons butter
2 tablespoons plain flour
sea salt and pepper
1 cup cream *or* milk
1 egg, beaten
½ cup grated parmesan

Preheat the oven to 180°C.

Peel the eggplants and cut into 1 cm thick slices. Heat the oil in a large, non-stick frying pan over medium heat and fry the eggplant slices until lightly browned. Drain on kitchen paper. Arrange half the eggplant slices in the bottom of a greased baking dish 23 cm × 23 cm.

In a large frying pan, combine the minced beef and onion and fry, stirring until the beef is browned and the onions are soft. Add the garlic, tomato, oregano, sea salt and pepper to taste. Stir through, then pour the mixture over the eggplant slices. Arrange the remaining eggplant slices over the beef mixture.

To make the cheese sauce, melt the butter in a saucepan and stir in the flour, plus salt and pepper to taste. Gradually stir in the cream until the sauce is thick and bubbly. Add the beaten egg and mix well, then add the parmesan and stir again.

Pour the cheese sauce over the eggplant in the baking dish and bake for 45 minutes.

To serve, cut the moussaka into squares and accompany with a green salad drizzled with extra-virgin olive oil and balsamic vinegar.

Simon Johnson is Australia's premier provider of quality food and food-related items, and is highly regarded for his ability to source quality artisan and mainstream products. He has Simon Johnson stores in Sydney's Castlecrag, Woollahra and Pyrmont, in Melbourne's Toorak and Fitzroy, and in Perth.

Potato and loukaniko scramble

Susie Theodorou

This was one of my mum Androulla's fast and easy weekday dinners. We always had elaborate Greek Cypriot meals at the weekends, especially for Sunday lunch, but this simple dinner was a family favourite. My brother and I would have eaten it every night if we had the choice.

Loukaniko is a spicy dried sausage made from pork, spices and red wine. You can find them in Greek delicatessens: they're a perfect larder staple.

Serves 4

1 kg large new potatoes

salt and pepper

olive oil, for shallow-frying

1 small onion, roughly chopped

4–6 (about 400 g) long, thin loukaniko sausages, cut into 1–2 cm pieces

6 eggs, beaten

2 tablespoons chopped flat-leaf parsley

Peel and wash the potatoes. Dry well, then cut into 2–3 cm chunks – the rougher the better. (Sometimes Mum cuts them into big fat chips!) Season with salt and pepper.

Pour oil to a depth of about 2.5 cm in a large, deep frying pan and place over medium–high heat. Test the temperature of the oil by adding one piece of potato to the pan – it should sizzle immediately. Add all the potatoes and cook for 15 minutes, stirring at least twice. The potatoes should start to crisp and turn golden brown on the outside, while the centres should be tender. Remove potatoes with a slotted spoon and place on kitchen paper for 5 minutes to drain further.

Meanwhile, drain off all but 2 tablespoons of the oil from the pan. Return the pan to a medium heat and add the onion and sausage. Sauté for 5 minutes, or until the onions just start to brown. Return the potatoes to the pan and stir to mix well. Increase the heat and add the eggs, tossing constantly so that the eggs set around the potatoes and sausage.

Spoon into a large bowl and sprinkle with parsley. Serve with a Greek salad.

Susie Theodorou is a freelance food writer and stylist based in the United States. She works on a number of publications, both there and in the United Kingdom, and regularly contributes to Australia's *Vogue Entertaining + Travel*. Susie's first book, *Coffee and Bites*, was published in 2001.

Moroccan salads

Margaret Fulton

Serves 4–6

Moroccan salad

2 red radishes, sliced or diced

1 continental cucumber, peeled, deseeded and diced

1 small red onion, diced or thinly sliced

salt

½ cup fresh mint leaves, torn

1 cup rocket leaves

1 clove garlic, peeled

2 tablespoons lemon juice

3 tablespoons extra-virgin olive oil

freshly ground black pepper

2 vine-ripened tomatoes

12 small black olives, pitted, to garnish

lemon wedges, to garnish

a few sprigs of mint, to garnish

Shredded salad

1 carrot

1 beetroot

½ large white radish

2 tablespoons lemon juice

4–5 tablespoons extra-virgin olive oil

1 teaspoon ground cumin

lemon *or* orange wedges, to garnish

Fresh salads precede most meals in Morocco. They are beautifully seasoned with unexpected flavours and contrasts. Such ingredients as carrots, beetroots and radishes are finished off with lemon juice (or sometimes orange juice) and a sprinkling of cumin. And, of course, good olives and olive oil are always in evidence.

Here are two salads that make an inviting platter when served together.

For the Moroccan salad, place the radishes, cucumber and onion in a salad bowl, sprinkle with salt and allow to stand for 5 minutes. Add the mint and rocket (you can cut the leaves in two if large).

Chop the garlic with ¼ teaspoon of salt. Transfer to a jug, stir in the lemon juice and olive oil and season with pepper, then pour this dressing over the salad. Toss the ingredients in the bowl, cover with plastic wrap and refrigerate for up to 2 hours.

Peel, deseed and dice the tomatoes. Stir them into the salad just before serving. Garnish with the olives, lemon wedges and sprigs of mint.

For the shredded salad, use one of the finest shredding blades of a plastic or wooden mandolin to shred the carrot, beetroot and radish, keeping them in separate piles. Make small mounds of each vegetable on a platter, pour over the lemon juice and olive oil and sprinkle with the cumin.

Serve with a garnish of lemon or orange wedges (some people like to squeeze extra juice over their salad).

Margaret Fulton is one of Australia's leading cookery writers. Her pre-eminence in the food world was given official recognition when she was awarded the Medal of the Order of Australia in the Queen's Birthday Honours of 1993. Margaret is a Governor (Honorary) of the University of Sydney Nutrition Research Foundation and a Patron of the Food Media Club. She was made a National Living Treasure in 1998.

Pasta
and rice

Linguini with blue swimmer crab, chilli, shallot and lemon

Peter Kuruvita

My mum, Leiselotte Katherina Kuruvita, always cooked pasta – it was a ritual. The varied types she produced never failed to amaze me. This dish is an accolade to my mum's cooking skills and a way of thanking her for instilling in me a passion to cook.

Serves 10

800 g plain flour
pinch of salt
4 eggs
8 egg yolks
100 g squid ink
⅓ cup olive oil

Sauce
1 cup olive oil
1 spring onion, white part only, finely chopped
1 small red chilli, sliced
800 g blue swimmer crab meat
6 cloves garlic, finely chopped
salt and pepper

Lemon oil
juice of 4 lemons
1 strip lemon rind
200 ml olive oil

To make pasta, combine the flour and salt into a food processor. Whisk the eggs, egg yolks and squid ink together in a separate bowl, then add to the processor.

Add the oil and pulse until the mixture just comes together. Tip dough onto a work surface and knead for a few minutes, then wrap it in plastic film and set aside for at least 30 minutes.

Using a pasta machine, roll out and cut pasta dough to make linguini. Place over a broom handle and cut into manageable lengths.

Cook pasta in boiling salted water, adding a small amount of olive oil.

While the pasta is cooking, make the sauce and lemon oil. For the sauce, heat oil in a frying pan over low heat and add the spring onion, chilli, crab meat and garlic. Heat through and season with salt and pepper.

To make the lemon oil, heat the lemon juice with the strip of lemon rind until the liquid is reduced by half. Whisk in the olive oil.

When the pasta is *al dente*, drain well, season and add a little extra oil to prevent the pasta sticking together.

To serve, use a fork to mould the pasta into individual bundles. Ladle the sauce on top of the pasta and dress with lemon oil.

Born in London to an Austrian mother and Sri Lankan father, Peter Kuruvita moved to Sydney with his family in 1974. In his early cooking–catering career he worked for renowned Sydney chefs such as Greg Doyle and Neil Perry, and was executive chef at Bilsons at Circular Quay for six years. He has since been chef in leading overseas hotels and resorts, and opened his restaurant Flying Fish, at Pyrmont, in 2004.

Gnocchi con ragu all'anatra (gnocchi with duck ragu)

Aldo Zilli

My mother had nine of us to feed, and this was one of the dishes she used to cook for us. She would cook the whole duck in the tomato sauce and then serve freshly made gnocchi with the sauce as a starter and the duck meat with a salad as a main. Delicious!

Serves 4

1 teaspoon olive oil
500 g duck breast fillets, diced
1 onion, chopped
1 clove garlic, crushed
4 tablespoons good red Italian wine
500 ml tomato passata
salt and freshly ground black pepper
flat-leaf parsley, to serve
freshly grated parmesan, to serve

Gnocchi
1 kg King Edward (or other floury) potatoes
salt
2 egg yolks
200 g plain flour
1 litre chicken stock *or* water

Heat the oil in a saucepan then add the duck, onion and garlic and cook for 10 minutes, stirring occasionally until browned. Deglaze the pan with the red wine and add the tomato passata. Bring to the boil and then simmer for 50 minutes over low heat until the meat is tender. Add seasoning to taste.

While the duck sauce is cooking, make the gnocchi. Cook the unpeeled potatoes in a saucepan of boiling salted water for 30 minutes, or until soft. Drain and allow to cool slightly. Peel the potatoes and mash or press through a potato ricer into a bowl. Season with salt, then beat in the egg yolks and flour, a little at a time. You should have a smooth, slightly sticky dough.

Tip the dough out onto a well-floured board, then roll the dough into long sausages about 1 cm thick. Cut into sections about 2 cm long. Place each piece on a fork and press down with your thumb and roll on the board, leaving grooves on one side of the gnocchi.

In a large saucepan, bring the stock to the boil and add the gnocchi, about 40 at a time. Cook until they rise to the surface, then cook for another 50–60 seconds. Remove with a slotted spoon to a large bowl, and keep warm while cooking the remaining gnocchi.

Pour the duck sauce over the gnocchi and combine lightly. Serve in individual bowls, topped with the parsley and parmesan.

London's renowned Italian chef Aldo Zilli grew up in a tiny village in the Abruzzo region and learnt to cook from his mother. He is the founder and chef patron of a group of popular restaurants, including London's first Italian fish restaurant, Zilli Fish in Brewer Street. He has won several awards, and makes regular radio and television appearances. He has written four cookbooks, runs a cookery school based in Abruzzo, and holds monthly master classes at Zilli 2 in London. www.zillialdo.com

Spaghetti bolognese

Gary Rhodes

Serves 4–6

1 tablespoon butter

1 large or 2 medium-sized onions, finely chopped

1 large or 2 medium-sized carrots, finely chopped

2 sticks celery, finely chopped

1 large clove garlic, finely chopped or crushed

2–3 glasses red wine

675 g beef fillet trimmings, coarsely minced or shredded

salt and pepper

freshly grated nutmeg

2 tablespoons olive oil

225 g tomato passata

1 teaspoon tomato purée

6 tomatoes, blanched, skinned and cut into 1 cm dice *or* 1 × 400 g can diced tomatoes

1 beef stock cube

Mum has always made (and still does) fantastic bolognese sauce. Here's her recipe, to which I've added a splash or two of Italian red wine.

Melt butter in a large saucepan and once it is bubbling add the onion, carrot, celery and garlic. Cook for a few minutes until the vegetables are slightly softened and coloured. Increase the heat and pour in the red wine (3 glasses leaves a much stronger finish), boiling until it reduces in volume by three-quarters.

While the wine is reducing, season the beef with salt, pepper and nutmeg. Heat the oil in a large non-stick frying pan, and when it is very hot fry the beef, a handful or two at a time, until well sealed and coloured. Add the beef to the vegetables, and pour in the tomato passata, tomato purée, and the tomatoes. Add 300 ml water, sprinkling in the beef stock cube. Simmer for 45–60 minutes, until tender and the sauce has thickened. Check for seasoning, and the sauce is ready.

A spoonful or two of this sauce over some tasty buttered pasta with freshly grated parmesan – you couldn't get more English!

Chef, television presenter and cookbook writer Gary Rhodes has played a significant role in reinvigorating British cooking over the last seventeen years. Television series like *Rhodes Around Britain* and *Gary Rhodes at the Table* have been hugely successful, as have Gary's various restaurants, earning Michelin stars and much acclaim.

Tagliarini con sugo di calamari

Guy Grossi

This recipe sticks in my mind because it was always cooked at Easter time. The whole family would fast on Good Friday until the afternoon, when we would sit down to a feast of seafood. The flavours were always so deep and comforting, and it was a real family time.

Sugo di calamari is characteristic of the northern Veneto region in Italy that Mum, Marissa Grossi, comes from. The sauce is rich and luscious, and once you have tried it you will be seduced for ever. I love it so much that sometimes I can't wait for the pasta to cook and eat a bowl of the sauce with some bread! I hope you enjoy it as much as we did.

Serves 10

2 tablespoons olive oil
1 onion, chopped
1 chilli, finely chopped
1 clove garlic, chopped
¼ bunch coriander, finely chopped
½ bunch parsley, finely chopped
6 tablespoons tomato paste
150 ml white wine
500 ml fish stock *or* water
salt and pepper
1 kg calamari, cleaned and cut into 1 cm thick strips
tagliarini pasta – allow between 100–150 gms per person

Heat 1 tablespoon of the oil in a frying pan and sauté the onion, garlic and chilli for a few minutes. Add the coriander and parsley and continue cooking until the onions are golden. Add the tomato paste and flour and cook until caramelised. Add the white wine to deglaze the pan, and allow to reduce. Add the fish stock or water, and season with salt and pepper. Keep warm over low heat.

In a separate frying pan, heat the remaining olive oil and sauté the calamari for 2–3 minutes or until it begins to change colour from clear to white. Add to the sauce and bring to the boil, then allow to simmer until well cooked and the sauce is reduced (about 45 minutes).

Add the pasta to salted, boiling water and cook until *al dente*. Drain the pasta and return to the pot. Add 2–3 large spoonfuls of the sauce and stir through. Serve in bowls with extra sauce.

Guy Grossi is the chef/owner of Melbourne's acclaimed Italian restaurant Grossi Florentino. In a career spanning more than twenty years, Guy has been a vigorous promoter of Italian cuisine in this country.

Ragu di Maria

Robert Castellani

This was a Sunday dish, a feast-day dish. The tomato sauce, or passata, was made at home and then bottled. The basil was home-grown.

My mother, Maria-Theresa Cincotta-Castellani, grew up in the south of Italy on the Aeolian Islands. When she married my father, who was a northerner, she went to live with my father's family on their rice farm. I grew up with the two cultures of Italy, the north and the south, and when we moved to Australia a third culture was introduced into my life.

This is a two-course meal. The sauce is added to pasta for a starter, then the meat rolls are served with a salad as a second course. At home we would have this dish not with pasta but with steaming soft polenta.

Serves 12

Meat rolls
12 small thin porterhouse steaks
salt and pepper
25 g freshly grated parmesan
4 cloves garlic, finely chopped
handful fresh flat-leaf parsley, torn

Sauce
½ cup olive oil
½ cup red wine
1 onion, very finely chopped
1 stick celery, very finely chopped
2 tablespoons tomato concentrate
or **tomato passata, diluted in 400 ml lukewarm water**
2 × 400 g cans diced tomatoes
salt and pepper
handful fresh basil leaves, torn

Arrange the pieces of steak on a chopping board or a clean work surface and flatten them with a meat tenderiser. Season with salt and pepper, then sprinkle with the parmesan, garlic and parsley. Roll up each slice tightly and secure well with toothpicks.

For the sauce, heat the olive oil in a large saucepan. When hot, lower the heat, add the meat rolls and seal well on all sides. Increase the heat again, add the wine and simmer until it has reduced by half. Remove the meat and set aside.

Add the onion and celery to the pan and stir well. Cook until the remainder of the wine has nearly evaporated, then return the meat to the pan and pour over the diluted tomato concentrate and the diced tomatoes. Season with salt and pepper and stir in the basil. Lower the heat and cover with a lid, but not completely, to allow some of the steam to escape. Cook for 2 hours, stirring from time to time. Check the seasoning.

Serve the tomato sauce with some cooked pasta such as tagliatelle or large rigatoni. Then serve the meat rolls as a main course with a green salad.

Robert Castellani was born in Pavia, Italy, and moved to Australia with his family at the age of six, travelling for six weeks by sea. He commenced his culinary apprenticeship at the legendary Fanny's Restaurant in Melbourne before moving to Stephanie's Restaurant where he worked for seven years, five of those as head chef. He now works at Donovans, one of Melbourne's most popular restaurants.

Pastitso (baked macaroni Greek-style)

Samantha Lee Douros

My husband is of Greek origin and I am of Chinese origin. This recipe is based on his mum's. When I first met my husband I found Greek dishes quite heavy compared to the lighter food I was used to. So I reduced the quantity of cheese and use low-fat milk in this traditional recipe. This version is a huge hit in our family, and my eight-year-old son eats a piece the size of a brick. It's a great family staple. Often I serve it with stir-fried vegetables!

Serves 4–6

Meat sauce
1 onion, finely chopped
1 tablespoon olive oil
1 tablespoon butter
500 g minced beef
1 × 400 g tin diced tomatoes
1 tablespoon tomato paste
½ teaspoon dried oregano
salt and pepper

Bechamel sauce
150 g butter
125 g plain flour
5 cups low-fat milk
2 egg yolks
salt and pepper

500 g macaroni or penne
¼–½ cup grated parmesan cheese

Preheat the oven to 180°C.

First make the meat sauce. Fry the onion in the oil and butter until soft and golden. Add the minced beef and fry until browned. Add the tomatoes, tomato paste, oregano, salt and pepper. Cover pan and simmer for about 30 minutes.

To make the bechamel sauce, melt the butter over low heat, sprinkle in the flour and stir for 1–2 minutes. Heat the milk and add it the butter–flour mixture, whisking continuously to avoid lumps. Bring just to the boil, then reduce heat and simmer for 5 minutes or until thickened and smooth. Remove from heat, mix in the egg yolks and season with salt and pepper.

Meanwhile, grease a rectangular ovenproof dish 22 cm × 36 cm. Boil the macaroni or penne in lightly salted water until just cooked, then drain.

Put half the cooked pasta in the greased oven dish, top with the meat sauce and then top this with the remaining pasta. Pour the bechamel sauce over the pasta, sprinkle generously with parmesan and bake for 45 minutes.

Samantha Douros is a third-generation Australian-born Chinese. Her grandparents, William and Jenny Wing-Young were fruit wholesalers who opened the Wing-Lee 'Chiko Roll' and dim sim factory. Her early life revolved around food and family celebrations, so when she married her Greek husband there was little change – just different food and a different language. She loves the flavours of Greece and combines them with Chinese meals to produce wonderful family dinners.

Rosa's lasagne

Laura Demasi

Serves 8–10

500 g plain flour, sifted

5 large eggs

1 tablespoon olive oil

100 g finely grated hard Italian
cheese (such as grana padano,
pecorine or parmesan)

100g mozzarella

Meatballs

500 g good-quality pork mince

2 cloves garlic, crushed

l tablespoon chopped parsley

4 large eggs

30 g fresh breadcrumbs

a good pinch of sea salt

black pepper, to taste

150 g finely grated hard Italian
cheese

Tomato sauce

1 medium-sized brown onion, finely
chopped

4 tablespoons olive oil

2 large cloves garlic, crushed

1.5 litres Italian tomato passata *or*
4 × 400 g cans tomato purée

6 large basil leaves

a good pinch of sea salt

freshly ground black pepper, to taste

My mother's lasagne is famous . . . well, at least amongst my family and friends. Growing up in the small mountain village of Martone in southern Italy, Mum (Rosa Demasi) was taught how to make lasagne by her mother, who was taught by her mother when she was a girl.

My mother has been making her special lasagne ever since I can remember, for Christmas lunch and other special occasions throughout the year. Making the lasagne is an epic project; it takes all day, starting with making the dough from scratch, preparing the meatballs and the tomato sauce, and eventually assembling the almighty thing. It's all about doing things the 'old way': making your own dough and, instead of using plain minced meat, making meatballs (which are infused with the flavour of a grana cheese and garlic) and then crushing them.

It's not the kind of recipe you should attempt on your own – it definitely requires a team effort. In that respect it's the perfect Italian meal – it's about bringing people together and sharing the experience.

Place flour on a clean work top, creating a well in the centre. Crack eggs into the well and add olive oil, and slowly blend into the flour using your hands until the mixture becomes a firm, smooth dough. Knead well for about 10 minutes. Wrap the ball of dough in plastic film and place in the fridge for 30 minutes.

Divide the chilled dough into 4 pieces. Using a pasta machine, roll the dough into sheets, gradually passing them through thinner settings until 1–1.5 mm thick. Place the finished sheets on a dry tablecloth lightly sprinkled with flour. The sheets may be up to 60 cm long; cut them into approximately 30 cm lengths.

To make the meatballs, put all the ingredients into a bowl and mix well with hands until combined. Coat your hands with water and roll the mixture into balls the size of a golf ball.

To make the tomato sauce, fry the onion in olive oil until golden brown, adding the garlic after a few minutes. Add tomato passata and bring to the boil, then reduce the heat, add the raw meatballs, basil, salt and pepper and simmer for 45–60 minutes. When the meatballs are cooked, remove them from the sauce and, using a fork, crush them until the meat is broken up.

Once the meatballs and sauce are ready, place the lasagne sheets in a large pot of boiling salted water (to which a tablespoon of olive oil has been added). Cook for 10 minutes, then remove from the pot with the handle of a wooden spoon and place flat on a dry tablecloth. ➤

Preheat the oven to 180°C.

To assemble the lasagne, select a ceramic baking dish about 25 cm × 35 cm and at least 7 cm deep and place a thin layer of cooked tomato sauce on the bottom. Place a layer of cooked lasagne sheets on top, trimming the sheets to fit. Add another thin layer of tomato sauce to coat the lasagne sheets, then sprinkle the crumbled meatballs on top, then some cheese. Add the next lasagne sheets and repeat until the dish is full. Make sure your last layer is lasagne sheets covered in a thin coating of sauce and cheese. Cover with foil and bake for 45–60 minutes, removing the foil for the last 5 minutes of cooking.

Coming from a big southern Italian family, Laura Demasi was predestined to be pre-occupied with all things culinary. From the earliest age she learnt from her mother, Rosa, that food was a feast for all the senses and that the ability to cook well was both a precious gift to be shared and celebrated and to be passed on to the next generation.

Quadretti e piselli (pasta with peas)

Maurizio Terzini

This is a very special dish that I grew up with. It is a traditional Abruzzese soup, not very glamorous but warming and comfortable. Today my mother prepares it for my son.

Fresh peas are really the best, but if they are out of season you can use frozen peas. Don't worry about the peas going slightly brown as they cook, as the taste is the most important thing.

Serves 4

2 large free-range eggs
sea salt
250 g plain pizza flour
virgin olive oil
1 kg fresh peas, shelled
1 brown onion, finely diced
salt and pepper
6 very ripe tomatoes
1 bunch parsley, roughly chopped
6 basil leaves, roughly torn
200 g parmesan, freshly grated *or* dried chilli, to taste

Beat eggs with a little sea salt. Heap flour onto work bench and make a well in the centre. With a fork, slowly mix in the egg and a teaspoon of olive oil to form a smooth dough. Roll the dough to around 5 mm thickness with a rolling pin or pasta machine, then cut the dough into little squares about the same size as the peas.

Place a skillet or frying pan over medium heat and add a little olive oil. Once warm (not hot), add peas, onion, salt and pepper and begin to sauté gently. While the peas are cooking, purée the tomatoes in a blender. Once the peas are tender (3–5 minutes), add tomato, parsley and basil, reduce heat to low and simmer for 15–20 minutes or until sauce has thickened.

Meanwhile, cook pasta in rapidly boiling salted water for 3 minutes or until cooked. Drain, reserving about 200–300 ml of the cooking water, and tip the pasta into the pea sauce. Adjust the seasoning if necessary and if the sauce is a little dry, add the reserved cooking water. Once ready, sprinkle with parmesan or dried chilli to taste.

Maurizio Terzini is one of Australia's leading Italian restaurateurs. With over a decade of hospitality success, he has created the Melbourne establishment Café e Cucina, The Melbourne Wine Room, Snakepit, Café Vini Spuntini and Il Bacaro, and Sydney's highly awarded Otto Ristorante, Nove Pizzeria and the acclaimed Icebergs in Bondi. His cookbook, *Something Italian*, was published in 2004.

Abacus beads (Chinese yam gnocchi)

Helen Pang

This specialty dish, which originated among the Hakka people (reputedly the wandering gypsies of the Chinese), is served during the Chinese New Year. I recall my mother preparing this dish for the family for the festive occasion as a symbol of prosperity and good fortune. Abacus beads are the Chinese equivalent of gnocchi. I have continued my mother's tradition and now serve them to my family during the Chinese New Year.

Serves 4

300 g yam *or* taro (I have often used frozen raw yam purchased from Asian grocery stores), peeled and finely chopped

300 g tapioca flour

50 g glutinous flour

½ cup water

salt and pepper

Sauce

2 tablespoons oil

2–3 cloves garlic

150 g minced pork

6 dried Chinese mushrooms, soaked until soft, then sliced

150 g dried prawns, soaked in hot water, drained and pounded

2 tablespoons oyster sauce

salt and pepper

chopped spring onions, fried shallots, 1 or 2 sliced chillies, and coriander leaves, to garnish

Steam the yam until soft. Allow to cool, then mash. Combine the flours, season with salt and pepper and add to the yam. Knead well until smooth, gradually adding the water.

Taking small amounts, roll the yam mixture into small balls. Flatten into discs about 1 cm thick, indenting both sides slightly. Bring a large saucepan of water to the boil and add the abacus beads, a small handful at a time. Cook until they rise to the surface, then remove and drain. Transfer to a bowl containing cold water (this prevents the abacus beads sticking to each other).

For the sauce, heat the oil in a large frying pan, add the garlic and fry until fragrant. Add the pork and fry until slightly brown. Add the dried mushrooms and prawns and continue to fry for a few minutes, or until all ingredients are cooked. Add the oyster sauce and salt and pepper to taste.

Next, stir in the drained abacus beads. (Add a small amount of water if the beads stick to each other.) Remove and sprinkle with spring onions and coriander leaves. Serve hot.

Helen Pang migrated to Australia from Singapore thirty-one years ago with her husband, Andrew. Drawing upon the diverse culinary influences of her homeland, she has since developed and refined her skills in the kitchen, cooking for appreciative family and friends.

Jollof rice (West African pink risotto)

Dorinda C. Hafner

Mum had a number of favourite recipes, but for me some are more memorable than others. Those which were prepared on special occasions in my life are indelibly etched in my memory. Jollof rice is one such recipe.

Just about every West African child has their version of Jollof rice. Mum's is like a member of our family; it remains a panacea for everything. It is present at every Christmas, Easter, birthday, engagement, marriage, christening and even at times of settling family disputes. It looks good, smells great, is easy to cook and is a clever way to transform simple ingredients into impressive exotica which feeds many and costs little.

Mum, you're a genius!

Serves 4–6

600 g lean beef *or* chicken thigh fillets

salt and freshly ground white pepper

1 cup corn or vegetable oil, for shallow frying

3 large red onions, finely chopped

4 cloves garlic, finely chopped

3 large red chillies or habaneros, seeded and finely chopped (optional)

4 large ripe tomatoes, blanched, peeled, seeded and blended

3 tablespoons tomato paste

1 cup each assorted chopped vegetables (such as carrots, green beans, mushrooms and capsicums)

1 litre beef or chicken stock *or* water mixed with 3 crushed stock cubes

3 cups long-grain rice (such as basmati or jasmine rice)

1 medium lettuce, sliced into thin strips, to garnish

fresh coriander leaves, to garnish

2–3 hard-boiled eggs, thickly sliced, to garnish

Cut beef or chicken into 5 cm cubes and season with salt and pepper. Cover and allow to stand for 2–3 hours. Heat oil in a frying pan and brown the beef or chicken in small batches on all sides until golden. Remove from oil, cover and set aside.

Drain excess oil from frying pan, leaving just enough (about ¼ cup) to fry onion, garlic and chilli (if used) until golden brown. Add blended tomatoes, tomato paste, half the chopped vegetables and all the stock. Stir well, taste and adjust seasoning. Add the meat to this vegetable sauce and simmer gently on low heat for 5–7 minutes. Stir in the rice, cover and simmer for about 10 minutes, then lift the lid and arrange remaining vegetables on top of the rice. Replace lid and continue to simmer for another 10–15 minutes, or until the rice absorbs all the stock, softens and cooks, and the meat is tender. It may be necessary to add extra stock or water to help the rice soften. (But remember, unlike Italian risotto the finished dish is dry rather than creamy, so if you do this use small amounts – e.g. ½ cup of stock or water at a time.) When the rice is cooked, fluff out with a fork. Serve risotto hot on a large platter, with some of the meat on top and garnished with lettuce, coriander leaves and hard-boiled egg.

Note: For special occasions, use chicken wings trimmed and formed into 'mini drumsticks'. You may also prefer to garnish the finished dish with a mixture of coriander leaves, cherry and yellow teardrop tomatoes, and edible flowers.

Dorinda Hafner has had a career in the arts, television and the food business for over twenty-six years. She has written seven books, two of them international bestsellers, and has fronted five television food-anthropology series. Currently, Dorinda is the Face of the Adelaide Central Market and is food and tourism ambassador for Food SA and the South Australian Department of Tourism.

Simple gorgonzola risotto

George Calombaris

My mother-in-law, Anna Bucciarelli, is a diva in the world of fine Italian cuisine. Not only do I enjoy the fruits of her gastronomy, but she has also inspired me to appreciate and learn about the simple things that create mouthwatering dishes.

The one recipe I have taken from Anna, and that I now use at Reserve every day, is risotto, made the proper Italian way. I not only enjoy making risotto but also eating it, as it reminds me of the celebration of food and family I experience every Sunday lunch at my in-laws.

Serves 2

1 tablespoon olive oil

¼ brown onion, finely diced

1 clove garlic, crushed

½ cup carnaroli rice

50 ml white wine

3–3½ cups chicken stock

20 g fresh broad beans, shelled

40 g gorgonzola

20 g unsalted butter

salt and pepper

Heat the oil in a heavy-based frying pan and sauté the onion and garlic until translucent. Add rice but do not stir; instead, shake the pan so the rice does not stick. Deglaze the pan with white wine, then add 1 cup of the chicken stock and keep shaking pan and adding chicken stock until all the liquid is absorbed and the rice is cooked (about 15–20 minutes).

Meanwhile, blanch the broad beans in boiling water for 2 minutes, drain, then chill at once in iced water. Slip the tiny bright beans from their skins.

Finish with crumbled gorgonzola and butter to give the rice a silky texture. Fold broad beans through, and season to taste with salt and pepper.

George Calombaris is chef de cuisine at Reserve, the flagship restaurant of the Victorian Wine Precinct at Federation Square in Melbourne. Previously, he worked at Fenix, which was Restaurant of the Year in the 2001 Culinary Competition for Victoria. George was named Young Chef of the Year 2004 by the *Age Good Food Guide*, which also named Reserve the Best New Restaurant 2004 and awarded it two chef's hats.

Main
courses

Blue grenadier with tomatoes

Fernando Cappelluti

Mum used to let me watch her while she cooked, as I always said I was going to be a chef. She taught me a lot, and as I got older I would have dinner prepared by the time she got home from work. This is one dish that I really enjoyed cooking. Sometimes we would eat it as an entrée, or Mum would add fresh home-made fettuccine and serve it as a main meal.

Serves 2

100 ml extra-virgin olive oil

5 cloves garlic, halved lengthways

6–8 large tomatoes, diced
***or* 800 g canned diced tomatoes**

ground chilli, to taste

¼ cup white wine

salt and pepper

500 g blue grenadier fillets

3 tablespoons chopped flat-leaf parsley

Heat the olive oil in a large frying pan over medium heat. Add the garlic and fry for 1 minute. Add the diced tomatoes, bring to boil and then let simmer for 5–8 minutes. Add chilli to your taste, then add the white wine and stir to mix. Season with salt and pepper to taste.

Place the fish fillets on top of the tomato sauce in the pan. Cover with a lid and let simmer for 20 minutes. Serve garnished with parsley.

Fernando Cappelluti started his apprenticeship with Brunetti Cakes in Carlton at the age of fifteen. He's now forty and still works at Brunetti – one of Carlton's defining and finest-quality eating establishments.

Fish cakes with tomato and herb butter sauce

Darren Simpson

Serves 1

This is the recipe for Irish fish cakes cooked by my mother, Sarah Simpson – made fancy!

100 g white-fleshed fish

1 large potato, cooked and mashed

1 small onion, finely chopped

1 spring onion (white part only), finely chopped

1 clove garlic, finely chopped

1 pinch ground red chilli

½ teaspoon each chopped fresh chervil, parsley and tarragon

1 egg, lightly beaten, to bind

salt and freshly ground black pepper

plain flour, to coat

1 egg extra, lightly beaten

breadcrumbs, to coat

4 tablespoons olive oil

Tomato and herb butter sauce

⅓ cup white wine

¼ onion, finely chopped

1 sprig each parsley and tarragon, chopped

1 tablespoon cream

100 g unsalted butter

salt and freshly ground black pepper

squeeze of lemon juice

1 small tomato, deseeded and chopped

chopped tarragon, to garnish

Poach the fish in a little water, white wine, salt, pepper and herbs. Combine the flaked cooked fish with the potato, onion and spring onion, garlic, chilli, chervil, parsley, tarragon and beaten egg. Season with salt and pepper and shape into 2 or 3 fish cakes. Dip the fish cakes in flour, egg and then breadcrumbs. Heat olive oil in a pan and fry fish cakes for 3–4 minutes each side, until golden brown. Keep warm while you make the sauce.

In a small saucepan, heat the white wine, onion, parsley, tarragon and cream until wine is reduced by half, then whisk in the butter and season with salt, pepper and a little lemon juice. Add the chopped tomato and tarragon, and serve with the fish cakes.

Irish-born Darren Simpson worked in London in a number of estimable restaurants, including a stint as head chef at Sir Terence Conran's Sartoria, and at twenty-one became the youngest-ever winner of the UK Young Chef of the Year Award. In 1999 Darren came to Australia to be head chef at Aqua Luna Bar and Restaurant at East Circular Quay, Sydney. Aqua Luna has consistently received acclaim for Darren's modern Italian cuisine.

Baked fish in paper

David Herbert

My mother, Noel Herbert, is a great fish cook. Where we lived when I was a child she had to be, as most days she was landed with an odd assortment of locally caught fish. I grew up in a fishing town on the coast of New South Wales and spent every spare moment fishing from the local jetty. Mum made wonderful home-made fish fingers and the best beer-battered flathead in the bay. But my all-time favourite, and the meal she most often made, was this simple dish of fish fillets wrapped in paper or foil and baked in the oven. Yum!

Serves 4

4 firm white fish fillets (such as snapper, blue-eye cod or jewfish)

sea salt and freshly ground black pepper

8 thin slices lemon

1 tablespoon chopped chives

30 g butter

1 lemon, quartered, to serve

Preheat oven to 200°C.

Cut 4 sheets of baking paper or foil 36 cm square. Place 1 sheet on your work surface and place a fillet of fish to the right of the centre. Season the fish well with salt and pepper and top with 2 slices of lemon. Sprinkle with a teaspoon of chives and add a knob of butter. Fold over the piece of paper or foil to enclose the fish, then fold the edges over twice to seal well, making a tight parcel. Mum used wooden pegs, or sometimes paperclips, to seal the parcels, and removed them before serving.

Repeat with the remaining fillets and place the parcels on a baking sheet, leaving space between each parcel.

Bake for 12–15 minutes, by which time the parcels should have puffed up a little. Transfer the parcels onto plates so they can be opened at the table.

Serve with lemon quarters and a good crisp, green salad.

David Herbert has been obsessed with food since he learnt to prepare his daily catch of fish in his grandfather's smokehouse at the age of eight. He is a weekly columnist for the *Australian*, from which derived *The Perfect Cookbook*, published in 2003, and *More Perfect Recipes*, published in 2005. He has contributed to numerous magazines, including *Australian Gourmet Traveller*, *Home Beautiful* and *Your Garden*. David is currently living in London, working for Delia Smith at *Sainsbury's Magazine*.

Whole steamed snapper with ginger and shallots

Kylie Kwong

There is nothing more tantalising and delicious than the smell of nutty, hot peanut oil scalding fine slices of ginger and shallots. This aroma reminds me of my youth – my mother, Pauline Kwong, would prepare steamed snapper with ginger and shallots twice a week. She would team it with her wonderful, silky soy-sauce chicken, fluffy egg and Chinese mushroom omelette, and a fresh stir-fry of bok choy with garlic.

Continuing my mother's tradition, I now serve this dish in my restaurant, billy kwong. It's a little bit like having Mum cooking with me in my kitchen every night! Other suitable whole fish for this dish are King George whiting, bream, coral trout, red emperor, Murray perch, silver perch or barramundi.

Serve as part of a Chinese banquet for 4–6

750–800 g whole snapper, scaled, cleaned and gutted

1 leaf Chinese white cabbage, cut into 4 squares

½ cup dry sherry

⅓ cup finely diced ginger

2 teaspoons sugar

3½ tablespoons light soy sauce

¼ teaspoon sesame oil

⅓ cup julienned shallots

¼ cup peanut oil

½ bunch coriander, leaves only

Pat fish dry and place on a chopping board. With a sharp knife, make three diagonal slits into the side of the fish. Turn the fish over and repeat on the other side.

Bring a large steamer pot of water to the boil. Arrange cabbage squares in a shallow, heatproof bowl and place fish on top. Pour sherry over fish, then sprinkle with half the ginger, avoiding the head. Place the bowl inside the steamer basket over boiling water, put the lid on and steam for 10–12 minutes, or until the fish is cooked. The flesh should be white through to the bone, which will be exposed by the cuts. If the flesh is translucent, replace the lid firmly and steam for another minute or so.

Remove steamer basket from steamer, then carefully remove the bowl from the basket. Sprinkle sugar evenly over fish, avoiding the head. Drizzle fish with combined soy sauce and sesame oil, and sprinkle with the remaining ginger and half the shallots.

In a small saucepan, heat peanut oil until it reaches smoking point. (Achieving the correct temperature is vital – the oil must be hot enough to 'scald' the ginger and shallots.) Slowly and carefully drizzle hot oil over the fish. Garnish with the remaining shallots, plus the coriander leaves. Serve immediately.

Kylie Kwong was born into a fourth-generation Australian–Chinese family. She learnt the fundamentals of Cantonese cooking at her mother's side before working at some of Sydney's finest restaurants: Rockpool, Wockpool and Restaurant Manfredi. Kylie then opened her own restaurant, billy kwong, in Sydney's Surry Hills. She has published two cookbooks, one of them, *Kylie Kwong: Heart and Soul*, coinciding with a television series that was screened on the ABC in 2003.

Crumbed fish

Peter Evans

I used to fish with my mum, Joy Johns, on the Gold Coast when I was growing up, catching flathead and bream. Even today I use fresh fish such as whiting for this recipe – there is nothing better.

Serves 4

½ cup plain flour

2 eggs, beaten

½ cup crumbled Corn Flakes

8 boneless whiting fillets

sea salt

⅓ cup canola oil

1 lemon, cut into quarters

chilli sauce (optional)

1 iceberg lettuce, cut into quarters

salad dressing made from lemon juice, olive oil and mustard

Place the flour, beaten egg and Corn Flake crumbs in three separate shallow bowls.

Lightly season the fish with salt, then dust the fish in the flour. Dip each fillet into the beaten egg and place into the crumbs, patting the crumbs on firmly.

Pour the oil into a large frying pan and place over medium–high heat. Fry the fish for 30–45 seconds on one side, or until golden and crispy, then turn and cook the other side for a further 30 seconds. Drain on kitchen paper and place on a serving plate with lemon wedges, chilli sauce (if you like) and dressed iceberg lettuce. Enjoy with a cold beer.

Originally from Melbourne, Peter Evans was head chef at The Pantry in Brighton and later established its hugely successful catering division. He went on to open Hugo's at Bondi Beach and Hugo's Lounge in Kings Cross, Sydney, and in 2004 Hugo's Pizzeria was born.

Flaky tuna and egg pie

Matthew Drennan

People have asked me if my passion for cooking came from my mother (Betty Drennan). Well, when I was growing up my mother cooked a meal for seven people three times a day and held down a part-time job. It didn't exactly leave much time for 'passion cooking'. While dinner wasn't always the most creative meal, it was always the best. This pie was one she cooked often and was always a winner with the family. With its crisp pastry and hot, creamy filling, it's easy to see now why kids loved it, and to be honest, I still do. Thanks, Mum.

Serves 4

50 g butter

50 g plain flour, plus extra for dusting

600 ml hot vegetable stock

salt and pepper

2 tablespoons freshly chopped parsley

4 hardboiled eggs, roughly chopped

1 × 400 g can tuna in sunflower oil, drained

500 g puff pastry

a little milk, for glazing

Preheat the oven to 210°C.

Melt the butter in a medium-sized frying pan and stir in the flour. Cook for 1 minute, stirring continuously. Gradually add the hot stock, stirring all the time, then cook for 5 minutes until thickened. Season well and stir in the parsley. Pour into a large, shallow container to cool quickly. Add the eggs and tuna to the sauce, then chill for 20 minutes.

Cut the pastry in half, then roll out one piece on a lightly floured surface until it measures 28 cm × 20 cm. Place on a baking sheet. Roll out the other piece to around 1 cm larger than the first piece. Spoon the filling on top of the base, leaving a 1-cm border all around, then cover with the other piece of pastry and press the edges with a fork to seal. Trim off any excess pastry. Brush the top with milk and bake for 30 minutes until golden and risen. (You can also make small, individual pies.)

Matthew Drennan trained as a chef in his native Cork in southern Ireland before moving to London to work in several top restaurants. He then became a food journalist, writing and creating recipes for national magazines including *Family Circle*, before launching *Ready, Steady Cook* magazine. He has written five cookery books and is currently the food editor of *delicious.* magazine in London.

Stuffed squid 'in umido' served with polenta

Loretta Sartori

The word *umido* is Italian for 'humid', and this expression denotes that the dish is 'wet', rather like a stew. The polenta is ideal for soaking up the rich sauces. We grew up eating polenta, as it is the staple of the Veneto region, from where my parents both come. We (my sister, two brothers and I) all learnt at an early age the appropriate action for stirring polenta with the aid of a wooden stick fashioned by my maternal grandfather. A copper pot purchased at the village market was used exclusively for cooking polenta. Most people from the Veneto have these pots in various sizes, depending on how many guests are expected at the table. Unlike richer recipes for polenta, we make ours with water and do not add cheese or any other flavourings.

Serves 4

1 kg squid (heads approximately 10 cm in diameter)

2 onions, finely diced

2 cloves garlic, peeled and pounded

1 cup good-quality breadcrumbs

¾ cup chopped flat-leaf parsley

⅓ cup olive oil

400 g ripe Roma tomatoes, peeled and diced *or* 1 × 400 g can diced tomatoes

200 g polenta

1 teaspoon salt

Remove the squid tentacles, pull out the cartilage and cut away the mouth and ink sac. Set the bodies aside. Pull the wings away from the head and remove the skin. Finely dice the wings and tentacles and place all in a bowl with half the onion and garlic. Add the breadcrumbs and half the parsley, and mix well. Using a small spoon, fill the squid body cavity with this mixture, pressing it in tightly, then seal the openings with robust toothpicks.

Heat the oil in a deep, heavy-based saucepan, add the stuffed squid and allow to brown before turning over. (Take care, as the squid will splatter in the hot oil.) Once the squid have coloured on both sides, add the tomatoes and remaining parsley, onion and garlic. Cover, bring to boiling point, then reduce heat and simmer gently for 30–40 minutes. If the sauce is too wet at the end of this time, remove lid and allow to reduce further.

While the squid is cooking, make the polenta. Bring 1 litre of water to the boil in a heavy-based saucepan and add the salt. Pour the polenta into the water, stirring continuously with a whisk. Reduce heat and exchange the whisk for a wooden spoon. Keep the heat low and cook slowly for at least 30 minutes, stirring every few minutes.

When cooked, spoon the polenta directly onto a wet serving dish (to prevent the polenta from sticking as it cools.)

Loretta Sartori trained and worked as a pastry chef in Melbourne and in Europe. She was the creative force behind the designer cake shop Distorta in Melbourne, and renowned for her dazzling celebratory confections. Loretta co-wrote *A Gondola on the Murray* with Stefano Di Pieri and has appeared on several television food programs. Her first solo book, *The Cooks Book–Patisserie*, was published in 2004.

Sardinas en escabeche (sardines in a traditional vinegar dressing)

Javier Codina

My mum, Encarna (her full name is Encarnacion Velasquez Bravo), has cooked this recipe for as long as I can remember. When I phoned her in Spain to ask for the recipe she started to cry, overwhelmed by all the memories associated with this dish. She remembered how, when my two brothers and I were kids, we used to go hunting for wild mushrooms and snails on the weekends. Mum used to prepare this dish for us the day before, to be eaten cold on our excursions.

You are very lucky to get this recipe out of my mum!

Coat the sardines in flour. Heat a frying pan with the olive oil and fry the sardines over high heat for about 2 minutes, or until golden brown. Set aside.

Combine all of the escabeche ingredients in a saucepan and boil for 5 minutes. Remove from the heat and add the fried sardines. They will be ready to eat the next day.

Javier Codina was born in Barcelona, came to Australia to take up the position of head chef at the Hayman Island Resort, and is now the executive chef at Gianni Restaurant and Wine Bar in Brisbane.

Serves 4

16 fresh West Australian sardines, butterflied
100 g plain flour
50 ml olive oil

Escabeche dressing
200 ml extra-virgin olive oil
50 ml sherry vinegar
50 ml white wine
1 teaspoon ground sweet paprika
1 head garlic, left whole and unpeeled
2 cloves
4 bay leaves
2 sprigs thyme
½ teaspoon sea salt
½ cinnamon stick
1 carrot, sliced
1 brown onion, sliced

Chicken karage (deep-fried my mum's way)

Tetsuya Wakuda

Serves 4

150 ml soy sauce

100 ml mirin

3 tablespoons grated ginger

2 cloves garlic, grated

2 pinches white pepper

1 pinch salt

1 teaspoon sugar

1 teaspoon sesame oil

500 g chicken thigh fillets, skin on, cut into bite-sized pieces

150 g plain flour

50 g potato flour

50 g cornflour

grapeseed oil *or* vegetable oil, for deep-frying

This dish reminds me of my childhood. Chicken karage is a very common dish in Japan, and my mother, Setsuko Wakuda, makes the best! Traditionally it is made with plain flour, but my mother mixes the different flours and this makes the chicken really crispy when cooked . . . and the chicken stays crisp, too. Chicken karage is still my favourite dish.

Combine the soy sauce, mirin, ginger, garlic, pepper, salt, sugar and sesame oil in a mixing bowl and whisk together thoroughly. Add the chicken pieces and toss to coat evenly. Cover and allow to marinate for 10–15 minutes.

Sift together the plain flour, potato flour and cornflour. Remove the chicken pieces from the marinade and dip into the flour mixture to coat evenly. When all the chicken is dusted with flour, set aside.

Meanwhile, heat oil in a deep frying pan to 170°C–180°C (use a thermometer to check). Fry the chicken pieces in batches in the hot oil until golden brown. Serve with a green salad.

Tetsuya Wakuda grew up in the Japanese town of Hamamatsu. At the age of twenty-two, and having only a limited grasp of English, he decided to travel to Australia. Seven years later, in 1989, he opened Tetsuya's in Sydney. He has since evolved his style and reputation to become a renowned chef both in Australia and overseas.

Mum's coq au vin

Ita Buttrose

When I was a very young bride my mother, Clare Buttrose, gave me her recipe for that old favourite, coq au vin. Since then I've cooked it countless times. Old-fashioned recipes are back in favour in the twenty-first century, and whenever I cook coq au vin, people invariably ask me for the recipe. Some people like mushrooms with their coq au vin. These should be sliced: I usually add them halfway through the cooking.

Serves 8

1 large chicken (preferably hormone-free), cut into pieces

2–3 tablespoons butter

6 thick rashers bacon

6 button onions, sliced

375 ml red wine *or* 185 ml red wine and 185 ml chicken stock

2 cloves garlic, sliced

1 bouquet garni

salt

1 tablespoon plain flour (optional)

2 tablespoons softened butter (optional)

finely chopped flat-leaf parsley

Preheat the oven to 180°C.

Heat the butter in a large pot and add the chicken pieces. Cook over low heat until brown, turning a few times. Remove from pot and set aside.

Meanwhile, remove the rind from the bacon and cut each rasher into three pieces. Place the bacon and onion in the pot and cook over low heat for 2–3 minutes, then return the chicken pieces to the pot and gently mix together. Add the wine, garlic, bouquet garni, and salt to taste, then cover and cook very slowly for 1 hour, or until the chicken is tender. (I usually cook coq au vin on the stovetop over low heat, but it is equally successful cooked in a casserole dish in the preheated oven for about 45 minutes.)

When the chicken is cooked, remove the bouquet garni. If you want the sauce to be thick, remove chicken from pot, mix flour with butter in a mug and then stir into the sauce. Return chicken to sauce and sprinkle with the chopped parsley.

Serve immediately with mashed potatoes, a green salad and crusty bread rolls.

Through her work in the media, particularly as editor of the *Australian Women's Weekly*, and for her involvement in various charity and welfare organisations, Ita Buttrose is one of Australia's best-known personalities. Currently she runs her own specialist publishing and public relations company, is editor-at-large for *OK!* magazine and is president of Arthritis Australia.

Jenny Lee's roast chicken

Elizabeth Chong

Family birthday dinners were always special when I was growing up as one of six children. The most important part of the birthday celebration was that Mum (Jenny Lee) would always make two of her special roast chickens.

I have eaten roast chicken all over the world and I swear I have never seen or tasted a chicken that comes even close to my mother's. Jenny Lee's roast chicken possesses a skin that is delicately crisp to the touch, with a colour like rich golden-brown honey. The flesh underneath that skin is so tender and moist that a butter knife could slice through to the heart. As children, the fragrant aroma of rice wine, soy, garlic and ginger wafting into the dining room let us know our special birthday treat was coming.

I've kept up Mum's tradition, cooking and presenting Jenny Lee's roast chicken at every family birthday dinner.

Serves 6–8

1 × 1.5 kg chicken
2 tablespoons white vinegar
2 tablespoons light soy sauce
2 teaspoons sugar

Stuffing
1 large clove garlic
3 slices ginger
1 spring onion
1 teaspoon sugar
1 teaspoon salt
2 teaspoons shao hsing rice wine
1 tablespoon light soy sauce

Take some kitchen string and tie a knot around the neck of the chicken to seal it up.

Now stuff the bird: put garlic, ginger, spring onion, sugar and salt inside, then add the wine and soy sauce and immediately sew up the rear end in blanket stitch. Alternatively, simply use several fine skewers at fairly close intervals to staple it closed.

Place the chicken in a strainer over the sink and scald it by pouring a large kettle of boiling water over the entire bird. The chicken will instantly swell up and firm out, and its skin will become satin-smooth and very tight.

Now, place the vinegar, soy sauce, sugar and 1 tablespoon water in a small saucepan and bring to the boil. Place a shallow dish or baking tray into the sink under the chicken and pour the hot marinade over the chicken. Recover the marinade, return it to the pot to boil and repeat the process another two times to ensure the entire skin has been treated. Never attempt to rub the marinade into the skin with your fingers, as this will cause unsightly blotches to appear after cooking. Moreover, do not be concerned if the skin doesn't change colour despite the use of the darkly coloured marinade. Oven cooking will soon do that.

Preheat the oven to 210°C. Place a metal grilling rack on the centre shelf of the oven and place a baking dish containing a small amount of water on the lowermost shelf. Carefully position the chicken on the rack, breast-side up. Roast for 10 minutes. Reduce heat to 180°C and cook for a further 30 minutes. Reduce heat again, this time to 150°C, and cook for a further 15 minutes. Take care not to overcook – the skin should be a chestnut colour, not dark brown. ➤

Remove rack with chicken from the oven, allow it to rest for 20 minutes, then remove the threads (or skewers) and string. Pour off any juices into a small saucepan ready for heating as a final dressing. Chop the chicken in the Chinese manner (through the bones into slices). Transfer onto a serving dish and spoon the dressing over.

This dish is best enjoyed *not* piping hot.

Born in China, Elizabeth Chong regularly appears on both television and radio and is well known for her books on Chinese cooking, as well as for her freelance newspaper and magazine articles. She is one of Australia's leading consultants to the Chinese food industry and runs Australia's premier Chinese cooking school, which she established in 1961.

Pheasant casserole

Louise Pickford

My earliest memories of food are always related to smell and I can still remember the rich pungent aroma of the pheasant casserole my mum, Elizabeth Pickford, used to make. Life on a farm meant we were mainly self-sufficient, with really wonderful fresh produce readily available. Pheasant, however, had to been hunted, and out of season this could be tricky – a little clandestine poaching was often resorted to. Mum's secret was to cook the birds in half milk and half stock, resulting in a thick, luscious stew. Rabbit can be substituted for pheasant.

Serves 4

a brace (pair) pheasants, about 500g each

4 tablespoons plain flour, seasoned with salt and pepper

2 shallots

6 rashers smoky bacon

350 ml game or chicken stock

350 ml milk

Stuffing

125 g fresh white breadcrumbs

1 shallot, finely chopped

1 tablespoon chopped fresh sage

25 g butter, diced

salt and pepper

Preheat the oven to 165°C. Wash and dry the pheasants, dust all over with the seasoned flour and pop a whole shallot into the main body cavity. Snip the rind from the bacon (reserve the rind) and lay 3 rashers over the breast of each bird.

To make the stuffing, place all the ingredients in a bowl and work together until just combined. Divide the stuffing between each bird, spooning it into the cavity along with the shallot.

Place the birds in a flameproof casserole dish and add the stock, milk and reserved bacon rinds. Heat gently over a low heat until the stock is just simmering, then cover with a lid and bake for 1½–2 hours until the meat is almost falling from the bones. Serve the pheasant with the pan juices and some roast potatoes, parsnips and carrots.

After working in London as a successful food writer and stylist, Louise Pickford moved to Australia in 2000 with her food-photographer husband. Louise lives and works in Sydney, where she is regular contributor to various food magazines. She is also the author of more than a dozen cookbooks, the latest of which, *Barbecues*, was inspired by her move. She loves Sydney's exciting, vibrant food scene, the high-quality Asian food, and the beach lifestyle.

Roasted goose with preserved lemon and liver stuffing, figs and caramelised garlic

Maggie Beer

Serving goose at Christmas has always been my sentimental favourite. As far back as I can remember, Mum cooked a banquet for Christmas and roast goose was always the centrepiece of the table. I have a 'dappled' memory of platters and platters of food, and often people we hardly knew were invited as Mum collected those who had nowhere else to go. When later we gathered with Colin's family at Mallala on Christmas Day, as lovely as it was to be there I so missed my own family traditions, that now goose is back in the centre of the table with glazed ham, ballottine of chook with mustard fruits, and other delicacies – always served banquet-style.

Serves 4

5 heads garlic
extra-virgin olive oil
1 × 2.5 kg goose
50 g unsalted butter
5 large ripe black figs (you can use dried figs out of season)
16 young sage leaves

Preserved lemon and liver stuffing
4 slices prosciutto
1 small onion, finely chopped
30 g unsalted butter
4 chicken livers
2 pieces preserved lemon, plus juice
1 tablespoon freshly chopped thyme
250 g fresh breadcrumbs
freshly ground black pepper, to taste

Preheat the oven to 200°C. Trim the tops from each head of garlic, then rub the garlic all over with olive oil and roast for 35–40 minutes, or until soft and caramelised. Set aside. Increase the oven temperature to 220°C.

To make the stuffing, crisp the prosciutto on a baking tray in the oven, then break it into small pieces. Reduce the oven temperature to 180°C. Fry the onion gently in the butter until softened. Trim the livers of any connective tissue and gently seal them in the same pan, then dice. Mince the preserved lemon and combine with the prosciutto, onion, liver, thyme and breadcrumbs. Season with pepper.

Pack the stuffing into the cavity of the goose, then rub the skin with juice from the preserved lemon jar. (This includes the oil from the lemon rind, which helps crisp the skin and gives it a delicious flavour.) Put the goose into an oven bag, seal and place in a deep baking dish. Pour ½ cup water into the dish and cook for 1 hour 20 minutes.

Take the goose out of the oven bag and increase the oven temperature to 230°C. Return the goose to the baking dish and roast for a further 20 minutes, then remove from the oven and allow to rest for 25 minutes.

Meanwhile, melt the butter in a saucepan until foaming and nut brown. Cut the figs in half and cook gently in the butter with the sage leaves for 3 minutes. Serve the roasted goose on a large platter with the figs, sage and roasted garlic to the side.

Maggie Beer operated the Barossa Valley's famous Pheasant Farm Restaurant with her husband, Colin, for nearly fifteen years. Since closing the restaurant in 1993, she has established a kitchen to develop and make specialised regional products for domestic and international markets. Maggie is the author of three successful cookbooks and co-author (with Stephanie Alexander) of another.

Coniglio al forno con prosciutto crudo e polenta (rabbit with Parma ham and polenta)

Giorgio Locatelli

This dish was my favourite from my grandmother, Vincenzina Tamborini, and it was passed on to her from her mother. My father used to breed rabbits and my grandfather used to choose the one that they would kill and cook. That might sound a bit shocking, but we were taught to respect animals and understand the responsibility of taking their lives away to feed others. These days, with packaged meat becoming more and more popular, most people seem to forget that the meat we buy might have been bred in conditions that were totally disrespectful to the animal.

Serves 6

6 rabbit legs, boned

12 thin slices Parma ham

2 tablespoons vegetable oil
or olive oil

50 g butter

500 g lard, melted

1.2 litres milk

sea salt

125 g polenta

2 heads radicchio

freshly ground black pepper

Preheat the oven to 120°C. Wrap each rabbit leg in 2 slices of ham. Heat half the oil in a large, shallow casserole dish and place the rabbit legs in it. Fry over medium heat until they start to colour, then add the butter. Turn the legs over and cook for a further 2 minutes. Cover the legs completely with the melted lard, then cover the casserole dish with foil and cook in the oven for 1 hour, or until the legs are very tender.

Meanwhile, cook the polenta. Bring the milk to the boil in a large saucepan; it should half-fill the pan. Add 1 teaspoon of salt and then slowly add the polenta in a continuous stream, stirring with a long-handled whisk all the time, until completely blended. The polenta will start to bubble volcanically. Reduce the heat as low as possible and cook for 20 minutes, stirring occasionally.

Cut each radicchio into 3 and season with salt and pepper. Brush with the remaining oil and cook on a medium–hot griddle pan until wilted.

To serve, spoon the polenta onto 6 serving plates and place the rabbit legs on top. Add the radicchio to the side and serve straight away.

Giorgio Locatelli was surrounded by good food from an early age, as his family ran a Michelin-starred restaurant in northern Italy. He worked in various restaurants in Italy and Switzerland before travelling to London to work first at the Savoy, then at Olivio as head chef. Giorgio opened his own restaurant, Zafferano, earning a Michelin star for his cooking. Later he opened Spighetta and Spiga, followed (in 2002) the Michelin-starred Locanda Locatelli.

Rabbit with fresh almonds

Theodore Kyriakou

My mother firmly believed that certain flavours were not for every day, and that having something all the time diminished its appeal. A perfect example of the pleasure to be had in the uncommon is this dish. And when nothing remains of the casserole but the memory of the green almonds, you are left glowing with a great happiness.

Serves 4

1 whole rabbit, skinned and cleaned

juice of 1 lemon

sea salt and black pepper

225 ml olive oil

200 g banana shallots (a longer, pale variety), finely diced

500 g fresh green almonds, still in the shell

700 g tomatoes, skinned, deseeded and finely chopped

1 bunch thyme, picked

60 g cold butter

120 g plain flour

120 ml white wine

220 ml chicken stock

Cut the legs off the rabbit and cut the back into three or four pieces. Keep the trimmings, offal and carcass. Wash the rabbit with the lemon juice and season with salt.

In a frying pan, heat 100 ml of the olive oil and sauté the shallots. When soft, add the almonds and tomatoes and simmer until the sauce starts to thicken (about 20 minutes). Remove pan from heat, add the thyme, adjust the seasoning and set aside.

In a heavy-based frying pan, melt the butter with 50 ml of the olive oil. Flour the rabbit portions and fry them over moderately low heat until they are cooked through. Turn the rabbit pieces a few times as they colour. As they are cooked (the back legs will take longer than the other portions), remove them from the pan and put them into the almond sauce.

Discard most of the oil, leaving only about ½ tablespoon in the pan. Flour all the reserved trimmings and offal and fry, turning frequently for a few minutes. Add the wine and increase the heat to allow most of the wine to evaporate. Pour in the chicken stock and reduce by three-quarters. Push all through a sieve to get maximum flavour out of the trimmings, and stir the resulting liquid into the pan with the rabbit and sauce. Simmer for 5 more minutes. Drizzle over the remaining olive oil and let the rabbit rest for 30 minutes. Serve with a warm salad of chickpeas and purslane.

Theodore Kyriakou was born in Athens and had a traditional Greek upbringing before moving to London to work as a chef. He is now chef/proprietor of the award-winning Real Greek Restaurant and Real Greek Souvlaki, both in London. He is the co-author of *Real Greek Food*, *Live Bait Cookbook* and *The Real Greek at Home*.

Roast beef with Yorkshire pudding

Sarah O'Hare

Roast beef with Yorkshire pudding always reminds me of our family getting together every Sunday night. Whenever possible we still do. No one's roast is as good as Mum's! Sometimes I make individual Yorkshire puddings rather than one large one.

Serves 6

1 × 2–2.5 kg beef scotch fillet *or* topside

canola oil

1 large onion

1 tablespoon plain flour

1 teaspoon gravy browning *or* Parisian essence

Yorkshire pudding
1 cup self-raising flour

1 egg

1¼ cups milk

Preheat the oven to 200°C. Put topside in a roasting pan and cover lightly with oil. Peel the onion and put in pan for flavour. Roast for approximately 1½ hours, or until done to your liking.

While the meat is cooking, make the Yorkshire pudding. In a large mixing bowl place the self-raising flour and make a well in the centre. Add the egg, then gradually add the milk. (The batter should be slightly on the thick side.) Let stand for 20 minutes.

Select a round pie dish and cover the bottom with some of the oil and juices from the cooked meat. Put in the oven to heat. Pour the batter into the hot dish and cook on the lowest shelf of the oven for 45 minutes, or until puffed and crisp.

When the meat is cooked, remove from the oven, transfer to a plate and leave to stand for 10–15 minutes.

Add the plain flour to the juices in the roasting pan, then add gravy browning or Parisian essence, and stir to blend. Strain some of the cooking liquid from any accompanying vegetables, or use hot water, and stir into the pan juices until the gravy thickens.

To serve, carve meat, cut Yorkshire pudding into wedges and arrange on plates. Serve with roasted potatoes, gravy and vegetables. Enjoy with the whole family!

Sarah O'Hare is a patron of the National Breast Cancer Foundation, the Australian Ballet and the McDonald College Foundation for Performing Acts, and ambassador for the Murdoch Children's Research Institute. She is also the spokesperson for Bonds. Sarah is currently studying for a degree in history and literature at New York University.

Wagyu beef and Guinness pie

Shannon Bennett

Makes 20 small or 1 large pie

50 ml olive oil *or* 100 g goose fat

1 stick celery, diced

1 carrot, diced

2 brown onions, diced

2 bay leaves

salt and pepper

2 cups Guinness

1 cup port

700 ml veal stock

800 g Wagyu beef silverside *or* chuck, diced finely

10 soaked prunes

200 g crushed hazelnuts

500 g puff pastry

1 egg

1 bouquet garni

¼ bunch parsley, chopped

30 g plain flour

Shortcrust pastry
250 g plain flour

150 g butter, cubed

1 egg

pinch of sugar

1 teaspoon salt

2 tablespoons milk

My mother, Bridie Bennett, was born in Dublin and raised with seven brothers and three sisters. Moving to Australia when she was nineteen, she has called it home ever since. Cooking has always played a huge part on both sides of my family, but my Irish heritage has influenced me greatly.

Mum's pie was based on my great-grandmother's interpretation of a French recipe, to which she added her signature detail of chopped prunes and hazelnuts. There was nothing better than coming home from a tough footy match on a Saturday to Mum's fresh beef pies and a glass of home-made ginger beer. (Wagyu is a flavourful beef from a Japanese breed of cattle, now available in Australia.)

Preheat oven to 150°C. Put the oil or goose fat in a heavy-based casserole dish with a lid, and sauté the diced vegetables and bay leaves over medium heat until soft. Season with salt and pepper (this will help the vegetables absorb the flavour from the goose fat, if using). Add the Guinness and port, reduce volume by half, then add the veal stock and reduce volume by a further third. Add beef, prunes and hazelnuts, then the bouquet garni, parsley and flour. Cover pot with foil and a lid, and place in preheated oven for 3 hours. Once cooled, leave this mixture to rest for 24 hours, covered, in the fridge.

To make the shortcrust pastry, combine the flour and butter with fingers to resemble breadcrumbs. Place in a food processor and quickly add the egg, sugar, salt and milk. As soon as the dough comes together, remove, wrap in plastic film and leave in the fridge for a few hours. Now roll out the dough to 5 mm thick. Place in an aluminium pie tin or moulds (for small pies use 6 cm moulds, for one large pie use a 30 cm mould). Trim edges and pack in filling to make a dome shape. Cover with two sheets of puff pastry: press the first one firmly over and trim the edges; cut the second into a lattice and arrange over the first layer, brushing a little water on first to ensure it sticks to the first sheet. Rest for a few hours in the fridge or freezer.

Brush pie with an egg wash made by combining the egg with a pinch of salt, and bake at 180°C for 25 minutes, or until golden. Serve with a hazelnut and watercress salad and a good glass of Australian shiraz.

Shannon Bennett began his culinary career at the age of fifteen, training at the Grand Hyatt Melbourne before moving to Europe and working in the kitchens of such greats as Albert Roux and John Burton-Race. For the last four years, however, Shannon's feet have been firmly set on home soil at his acclaimed Melbourne restaurant Vue de monde. His first cookbook, *My Vue*, was published in 2004.

Polpettone al sugo (meat loaf in tomato sauce)

Antonio Carluccio

My mother, Maria Crivellone, used to cook this during the war, when you couldn't find a nice piece of beef with which to prepare a ragu. Minced meat was both available and economical, and I distinctly remember how this dish used to satisfy our appetites. It had two advantages: the sauce in which the meat loaf was cooked provided an excellent dressing for pasta, which was served up as a first course; then the meat loaf, cut into slices, appeared as a tasty main course.

Serves 8

1 kg minced beef

175 g fresh breadcrumbs

2 tablespoons finely chopped flat-leaf parsley

55 g freshly grated parmesan

salt and pepper to taste

4 eggs

olive oil, for frying

Tomato sauce

1 onion, chopped

1 clove garlic, chopped

⅓ cup olive oil

2 × 800 g cans peeled tomatoes, drained of some of their liquid

salt and pepper

10 fresh basil leaves, torn

Mix the minced meat together with the breadcrumbs, parsley and parmesan, season with salt and pepper and mix thoroughly. Lightly beat the eggs and add to the mixture, which should now stick together. Fry a small meatball to check the seasonings. Form the mixture into a large, oval-shaped loaf. If you have difficulty shaping it and it is falling apart, add a few more breadcrumbs to the mixture.

In a large, oval cast-iron casserole dish, heat the olive oil and fry the meat loaf until it is crisp and golden brown all over and retains the juices of the meat inside. Take great care not to break the loaf as you turn it in the casserole. Set aside.

Now make the tomato sauce. In a separate frying pan, fry the onion and garlic in the olive oil for a few minutes, add the tomatoes and let simmer for 20 minutes. Season with salt and pepper, and add the basil.

Now add the sauce to the meat loaf, put the lid on the casserole dish and return it to the stovetop. Simmer gently for 1 hour, gently turning the loaf from time to time. Remove the lid after 30 minutes to allow the sauce to thicken. (This cooking process can also be done in the oven at 200°C.)

When the loaf is cooked, use the rich tomato sauce to dress some pasta. The meat loaf should be allowed to cool for 10 minutes before it is sliced, and is nicest served with fried potatoes.

Antonio Carluccio was raised on genuine Italian food. He is the author of several best-selling cookbooks and the host of a highly successful cooking series in the United Kingdom. Since 1999 he has also opened a number of food stores there, supplying regional Italian produce and products.

Chilli con carne

Teage Ezard

Serves 4

All I remember of coming home each Sunday night after a weekend's sailing at the Brighton Yacht Club in bayside Melbourne is the smell of my mum Bernadette Ezard's chilli con carne and the home-made garlic bread accompanying it. It was always so good to be home.

2 tablespoons oil

500 g minced topside beef

250 g pork *or* veal mince

1 large onion, finely chopped

2 cloves garlic, crushed

280 ml beef stock, heated

3 large tomatoes, peeled and diced

1 bay leaf

½ teaspoon finely chopped oregano

salt and pepper

½ teaspoon ground chilli

1 teaspoon plain flour

1 × 400 g can kidney beans

Heat the oil in a large frying pan and cook the beef and pork or veal mince over medium heat until brown. (It's best to do this in batches.)

Return all meat to the pan and add the onion and garlic. Cook for 5–10 minutes. Drain off fat, add most of the heated stock and bring to the boil. Cover the pan and simmer for 1 hour. Add tomatoes, bay leaf, oregano and salt and pepper to taste. Mix ground chilli and flour with the remaining hot stock, then blend into the meat mixture and bring back to the boil. Cover and simmer for a further hour.

Adjust seasonings, add kidney beans and heat through. Serve with garlic bread.

Teage Ezard is one of Australia's most exciting chefs. He opened his award-winning restaurant, ezard at adelphi, in 1999, and it is now regarded as one of Melbourne's finest. He was named Chef of the Year by the *Age Good Food Guide* in 2003, in which year he also released his first cookbook, *ezard*.

Oxtail stew

Terry Durack

I am never happier than when I am slurping up sauce and meat from the bone – any bone, be it lamb shank, pork rib, chump chop, veal chop, ham hock, osso buco or oxtail. Especially oxtail. My stew dependence can be traced directly back to my mum Ivy Durack's oxtail stew, which used to turn up on Tuesday nights on a pretty regular basis. As a pub cook, she had a talent for turning the cheapest cut of meat into the stew of your dreams.

This is my version of her oxtail stew. It's close, but not quite as sticky, messy, gloopy or glorious as hers. Mum always served it with mashed potato, which was my second favourite thing to eat.

Serves 4–6

2 oxtails, cut into joints
2 tablespoons plain flour
salt and pepper
2 tablespoons melted butter
2 tablespoons olive oil
2 onions, halved and sliced
2 thick rashers bacon, chopped
2 cloves garlic, minced
1 cup red wine
1.5 litres chicken *or* beef stock
6 peppercorns
2 bay leaves
6 sprigs thyme
2 carrots, peeled and chopped
2 turnips, peeled and chopped
chopped fresh parsley, to garnish

Roll oxtail pieces in flour seasoned with salt and pepper. Brown them in the melted butter and olive oil in a large saucepan, then remove from the pan. Add the onion (adding more oil if necessary), and cook until golden. Add the bacon and garlic, and cook gently for a couple of minutes. Return the oxtail to the pan. Pour in the wine and, over high heat, reduce the liquid by half. Add the stock, peppercorns, bay leaves and thyme. Bring to the boil and skim the fat from the surface. Cover and simmer gently for 1 hour. Add the carrot, turnip, salt and pepper, and continue to simmer for a further 2–2½ hours.

Check the seasoning, scatter with parsley and serve with plenty of mashed potatoes.

Terry Durack is a noted restaurant reviewer and food columnist. He contributes to several international journals and guides, and is the author of *Yum* and *Noodle*, co-author of *Hot Food Cool Jazz* and *Allegro Al Dente*, and is a former co-editor of the *Sydney Morning Herald Good Food Guide*. He lives with his wife, Jill Dupleix, in London.

Steak and onion casserole

Ross Dobson

Although Mum (Carmel Dobson) does just about everything else around the house, my dad considers himself the cook in the family. This recipe comes from *his* mum (who is ninety-seven and still has a very healthy appetite) and has its origins in the 1930s and '40s.

The original recipe calls for blade steak cut from the bone (the bone can later be used for soup) and also for Marmite and suet. I have always loved Marmite and have included it as an ingredient, but I drew the line at suet.

Serves 6

1.5 kg blade steak, cut into 4–5 cm pieces

½ cup plain flour

50 g butter

2 tablespoons olive oil

4 brown onions, cut into ½ cm thick slices

½ cup red wine

2 cloves garlic, peeled

1 × 400 g can peeled tomatoes

1 tablespoon Marmite

1 tablespoon Worcestershire sauce

salt and black pepper

Preheat oven to 180°C. Place the steak in a large bowl with the flour and toss around to evenly coat the pieces.

Heat the butter and 1 tablespoon of the olive oil in a casserole dish over medium heat. When the butter begins to sizzle, add half the steak pieces and cook for 2 minutes each side, or until nicely browned. Place the cooked meat on a plate and repeat with the remaining steak. Remove to the plate with the other cooked steak.

Add the remaining oil to the pan and cook the onions over medium–low heat for 5 minutes, or until they just begin to soften. (Keep the saucepan lid on but stir often.) Increase heat to high and add the red wine. Cook for 1 minute, then return the beef to the pan with the garlic, tomatoes, Marmite and Worcestershire sauce. Season with salt and black pepper and pour over 1 litre of water. Stir well for a minute to combine all ingredients. Place a lid on the saucepan and put in the oven for 1 hour, then give a good stir, remove the lid and continue cooking for a further 1 hour.

Serve with creamy mashed potatoes. Any leftovers are great the next day over thick, buttered slices of toast.

Chef and food stylist Ross Dobson has contributed to some of the most beautiful food books published in Australia and overseas. His unique approach to food is captured in his own book, *Chinatown*, published in 2005, which explores the wonderful range of ingredients available in the Chinatowns of many cities, from Melbourne to Mumbai. Ross also contributes to a weekly food column in a Sydney newspaper.

Slow-braised cumin-crusted lamb shoulder with carrot purée

Peter Gilmore

Whenever I go home to visit Mum and Dad, it is the slow-cooked braises and roasts – which my mum, Dawn, cooks like nobody else! – that transport me back to childhood. The aromas and flavours are linked to a sense of nurture and love.

My mother's passion for cooking inspired me from a young age. Her sense of care, and her investment of love and time in the special meals she would cook for the family, have always reminded me of how important it is to cook from the heart. I've adapted this dish from one of my mum's slow-cooked braises. Take the time to make a nice home-made chicken stock. You can make it in advance and freeze it.

Serves 6–8

2 tablespoons cumin seeds

180 g butter

1 young lamb shoulder, bone in

sea salt

50 ml olive oil

4 litres chicken stock

10 carrots (select the sweetest ones you can find)

10 shallots

3 cloves garlic

Preheat oven to 110°C.

Dry-roast the cumin seeds in a heavy-based frying pan over medium heat until they are lightly coloured. Place the seeds on a chopping board and, with a large knife, chop until they are as fine as sand. Rub 30 g of the butter into the lamb shoulder, then rub in the cumin and a couple of pinches of salt.

Select a lidded, heavy-based braising dish in which the lamb will fit snugly. Add the olive oil and heat on top of the stove. Add the lamb and sear on all sides. Pour in enough chicken stock to cover the lamb by at least 3 cm. Place the lid on the dish and cook in the oven for 6 hours. Keep an eye on the lamb to make sure that the meat is still just covered with stock – if not, add a little more stock and replace the lid.

An hour before your lamb is ready, prepare your carrot purée. Peel the carrots, shallots and garlic and cut the carrots into 2 cm pieces. Leave the garlic cloves and shallots whole. In a heavy-based saucepan, melt 50 g of the remaining butter and sauté the carrots over medium heat until they are well coloured. Add the garlic and shallots and sauté for a further minute. Add enough chicken stock to just cover the carrots, then cook slowly over medium heat until almost all of the stock has evaporated and the carrots are very soft. Place the carrots (with the remaining cooking juices), shallots and garlic into a food processor, add another 50 g of butter and blend well. Pass the purée through a fine sieve, if you like, or leave as is. Season with salt.

Carefully remove the lamb (which should be very tender and just about falling off the bone) with a couple of sturdy spatulas and place on an appropriate-sized plate. Cover with foil to keep warm. Increase oven temperature to 180°C.➤

Strain the remaining stock into a saucepan. Remove the surface oils with a ladle and reduce the stock over high heat until you are left with about 500 ml of reduced stock. Melt the remaining butter into the boiling stock to form a rich sauce.

Carefully remove the bone from the lamb shoulder – it should just twist out. Place the lamb back into the braising dish and pour over the sauce. Return dish to oven for 5–10 minutes, basting the lamb with the stock several times.

To serve, reheat the carrot purée and place in a warmed serving bowl. Serve the lamb in its braising dish. The meat should be soft and tender enough to serve with a spoon. Share with family or friends and enjoy your efforts!

Born in Sydney, Peter Gilmore is the executive chef at Quay restaurant, which was awarded three chef's hats and named Restaurant of the Year in the 2003 *Sydney Morning Herald Good Food Guide*. He has been awarded three chef's hats three years in a row and taken out the Restaurant of the Year again in the 2005 *Sydney Morning Herald Good Food Guide*.

Meat pies

Donna Hay

My mum Judy's meat pies were a weekend favourite in our house – the perfect winter warmer. The two pastries – shortcrust for the base, puff for the top – the rich meat filling, a dollop of tomato sauce . . . they were the best. No matter how many times I've tried to copy her recipe, my pies never taste quite like hers. Maybe because some recipes are meant stay a mum's secret.

Makes 6 pies

1 tablespoon oil
2 onions, chopped
1.5 kg round or chuck steak, cut into 1.5 cm cubes
1 tablespoon tomato paste
4½ cups beef stock
1 cup red wine
1 tablespoon Worcestershire sauce
2 tablespoons cornflour
¼ cup water
sea salt and cracked black pepper
350 g shortcrust pastry
375 g puff pastry
1 egg, lightly beaten

Preheat the oven to 180°C.

To make the pie filling, heat the oil in a saucepan over high heat. Add the chopped onion and cook for 2 minutes or until soft. Add the meat and cook for 5 minutes or until sealed. Add the tomato paste, stock, wine and Worcestershire sauce to the pan and simmer, uncovered, for 1 hour or until the meat is tender.

Blend the cornflour and water to a smooth paste. Add to the beef mixture and stir for 4 minutes or until the mixture has thickened and returned to a simmer. Add the salt and pepper, then set aside to cool.

Roll out the shortcrust pastry on a lightly floured surface to 3 mm thick. Cut out six pie bases (you may need to re-roll the scraps) to line pie tins 9 cm (base) × 11 cm (top). Spoon in the filling. Now roll out the puff pastry until 3–4 mm thick and cut out six lids. Lay over the filled pie bases, trim and then press the edges of the pastry together. Brush the tops with the beaten egg and make a slit in each pastry lid. Bake for 30 minutes or until golden.

Donna Hay's relaxed approach to food and her fresh, modern cooking style have become a benchmark for cooks around the world. Since 1997 she has written eight phenomenonally successful cookbooks (including the *marie claire* series, plus *off the shelf* and *modern classics book 1* and *book 2*, and *the instant cook*) and produces the bi-monthly *donna hay* magazine. She has a weekly column in Sunday editions of News Ltd newspapers around Australia and for *The New Zealand Weekend Herald*.

Mishmisheeya (Syrian stuffed kibbeh)

Greg Malouf

Kibbeh are those little torpedo-shaped meat dumplings that, once upon a time, were the yard-stick by which all Middle Eastern cooks were judged. They are a speciality of Syria and Lebanon, where marriages have been made and reputations destroyed, according to the skill of the cook. My mum, May Mary Malouf, made the traditional version: it consists of a thin crispy shell made of burghul and lamb, which is stuffed with a finer mixture of spiced lamb. Mum's mishmisheeya achieved legendary status in the Malouf household. My very untraditional version has a surprise filling of cinnamon butter and pine nuts, and to be quite honest they are a little fiddly to make. But you don't really require years of apprenticeship to a Lebanese housewife to achieve a passable (exceptional, even) result, and they are fun!

Serves 6 (3 pieces per person)

150 ml olive oil, for frying the kibbeh

Kibbeh shell
150 g fine-grade white burghul (cracked wheat)

400 g double-minced lamb

1 onion, puréed in a food processor

¾ teaspoon allspice

½ teaspoon ground cinnamon

¼ teaspoon chilli powder

sea salt and pepper

Filling
250 g softened unsalted butter

100 g pine nuts, fried in olive oil until golden

1 teaspoon ground cinnamon

sea salt

To make the kibbeh shell, begin by soaking the burghul in plenty of cold salted water for about 10 minutes. Using your hands, squeeze out as much water as you can, then tip into a tea towel and twist to extract even more.

Put the lamb in a large mixing bowl with the onion, burghul and all the spices, and add salt and pepper to taste. Use your hands to squeeze and mix everything to a soft, smooth paste. (You may need to add a few tablespoons of cold water to help bind the mixture together.) Refrigerate for 30 minutes.

While the lamb paste is chilling, prepare the filling by blending the butter with the pine nuts, cinnamon and salt to taste. Roll in plastic film, forming a long tubular shape as thick as a 20-cent piece. (This quantity will make much more than you need, but any left over can be used later on grilled fish or poultry.)

Take a small lump of the lamb paste (about 60 g) into the palm of one hand and roll it into a smooth ball. Using the forefinger of your other hand, make an indentation in the lump and start to shape it into a hollow shell. Try to make the shell as thin and even as you can. Fill the shell with about a 3 mm slice of the pine nut stuffing, then wet the edges of the opening with cold water and pinch it closed. Repeat with the remaining lamb paste and filling. You are aiming for small, hockey-puck-like discs. Leave the stuffed kibbeh on a tray, covered, in the refrigerator until you are ready to cook them.

Heat the oil in a frying pan to medium. Shallow-fry the kibbeh in batches for 1½–2 minutes on each side, turning to ensure a deep golden-brown colour all over. Drain on kitchen paper. ➤

Yoghurt sauce

1 heaped teaspoon cornflour

2 cups plain yoghurt

1 egg, beaten

1 litre chicken stock

1 cup cooked risotto rice

180 g cooked chickpeas

1 cup blanched and chopped spinach

½ cup chopped coriander

sea salt and white pepper

1 pinch allspice

juice of 1 lemon

To serve

salad of herb leaves (a mix of coriander, parsley, mint and parsley), seasoned with salt and pepper

seeds from 1 pomegranate

100 ml extra-virgin olive oil

To make the yoghurt sauce, blend the cornflour with ½ cup of cold water and add to the yoghurt and egg. Place chicken stock in a saucepan together with rice, chickpeas, blanched spinach and coriander and cook gently for 5 minutes. Then add the yoghurt sauce. Season with salt, pepper, allspice and lemon juice.

To serve, pour yoghurt sauce into shallow soup bowls and place kibbeh on top. Garnish with a little herb salad, some pomegranate seeds and a drizzle of extra-virgin olive oil.

Drawing on his Lebanese cultural heritage and his passion for the flavours of North Africa and the Middle East, Greg Malouf has forged a unique style of cooking – one recognised by numerous industry awards. He has published two cookbooks, *Arabesque* and *Moorish*, and has launched his own range of spice blends, called Spice Mezza. He is currently chef at Mo Mo, one of Melbourne's finest restaurants.

Baked ham

Joan Campbell

My mother Beatrice Perry (née Grigor) was born in Scotland. She cooked very well, and our family meals were always delicious as well as wholesome. This recipe was taught to Mother by her great friend and neighbour Gladys Dobell, an American who lived opposite us in Brisbane.

Serves 12

440 ml pineapple juice (canned is fine)

¼ cup sherry

500 g brown sugar

1 leg of cooked ham

approximately 3 tablespoons English mustard

3 teaspoons ground cloves

Preheat oven to 150°C.

Put the pineapple juice, sherry and brown sugar in a saucepan and cook to a syrup.

Carefully remove the skin from the ham and rub in the mustard to colour the fat bright yellow. Dust lightly with the ground cloves.

Place the ham in a large roasting tray and pour the syrup around the ham – not on top of it. Cook on the bottom shelf of the oven for 30 minutes. Then, basting with the syrup every 15 minutes and turning the pan, cook for a further 1 hour.

Serve hot or cold.

Joan Campbell is Food Editor at Large for *Vogue Entertaining and Travel*. She was food editor for Condé Nast Publications (*Vogue Australia*, *Vogue Living* and *Vogue Entertaining*) for twenty-five years and has contributed to magazines and newspapers around the world as a food writer and restaurant reviewer. She has produced three cookbooks: *Bloody Delicious*, *Five Minutes in the Kitchen* and *From Market to Table*, the last co-produced with Barry MacDonald.

Orange and coriander roasted loin of lamb

Janet Jeffs

This recipe is one which Mum, Shirley Jeffs, makes as a special treat and is usually requested as a birthday dinner. Mum is into growing herbs – coriander, basil and mint are favourites – so they are often at hand for making stuffings to jazz up roasts, or to add to everyday pasta dishes.

Serves 4

1–1.2 kg boned lamb loin, trimmed of skin and fat (to allow 200 g per person)

2 tablespoons ground toasted coriander seeds

Stuffing
30 g butter

1 small onion, finely diced

zest and juice of 1 orange

120 g coarse breadcrumbs

½ bunch fresh coriander, chopped

1 egg, beaten

Gravy
1 tablespoon plain flour

375 ml lamb, chicken *or* beef stock

Preheat oven to 180°C.

To make the stuffing, heat the butter in a heavy-based frying pan and cook the onion over low heat until soft but not coloured (about 5 minutes). Mix orange juice and zest with the cooked onion, breadcrumbs, coriander and half the beaten egg.

Lay the lamb loin out flat, boned side uppermost (you may need to pound it a little to flatten and broaden it). Spoon the stuffing along the meat, near where it meets the flap. Roll up meat to form a long cylinder, then secure with kitchen string at 5 cm intervals.

Place the meat on a rack in a roasting tray and bake for 40–50 minutes (or 20 minutes per 500 g). Remove from oven, brush with the remaining beaten egg and roll in ground coriander, then return to the oven for a further 3–4 minutes to form a spice crust. Remove lamb from the oven and let it rest in a warm place for 5–7 minutes.

While the lamb is resting, make the gravy by draining all but 1 tablespoon of the juices from the roasting tray. Sprinkle the tray with flour and mix with the juices, then cook over low heat to colour the flour, slowly adding stock while stirring. Simmer for 5 minutes to cook the flour and slightly thicken the gravy.

Carve the lamb into rounds, allowing 2 slices per person, and place on warmed plates. Strain the gravy and pour over the lamb slices, and serve with roasted vegetables.

Janet Jeffs opened Canberra restaurant Juniperberry in 1995 and it was awarded a chef's hat in the *Sydney Morning Herald Good Food Guide* every year thereafter. Janet moved Juniperberry to the National Gallery of Australia in 2000 and then, in partnership, established Ginger Catering at Old Parliament House. Janet opened The Ginger Room in March 2004 and it was awarded a chef's hat in the 2005 *Sydney Morning Herald Good Food Guide*.

Lamb shanks with braised vegetables and mashed potato

Matt Moran

Lamb is one of my favourite ingredients to cook with, especially in winter. This recipe is heavily based on a dish Mum (Carolyn Moran) made, but I have adapted it slightly to include more herbs, adding even more flavour. I always remember Mum using fresh ingredients from our garden.

Serves 6

3 tablespoons olive oil

12 lamb shanks

2 small brown onions, diced

1 stick celery, diced

3 carrots, diced

5 cloves garlic, chopped

leaves from ½ bunch thyme

2 teaspoons roasted coriander seeds

2 teaspoons roasted cumin seeds

5 threads saffron

300 g Sharwood's green label mango chutney

1 bay leaf

500 g Roma tomatoes

400 ml red wine

600 ml chicken stock

300 g mashed potatoes, to serve

250 g blanched garden peas, to serve

Heat the oil in a large pot, add the lamb shanks and cook until brown on all sides. Remove the shanks and set aside.

Add the onion, celery and carrot to the casserole pot and sauté until tender, then add the garlic, thyme, coriander seeds, cumin seeds, saffron, chutney, bay leaf and tomatoes. Sauté for 2 minutes, then add the wine and stock and bring to the boil. Return the lamb shanks to the casserole. Simmer for 3 hours, or until tender (the lamb should be just falling off the bone).

Strain the lamb shanks and vegetables, then pass the remaining liquid through a very fine sieve. Return the liquid to the pot and heat to just below boiling to reduce volume by half. Skim off any fat from this reduction. Once reduced, return the shanks and vegetables to the casserole dish and keep warm, ready to serve.

To serve, place some mashed potato in the middle of each plate and spoon the vegetables and sauce on top. Arrange 2 lamb shanks over the vegetables and then finish by scattering some peas around the plate.

Former country boy Matt Moran began his working life with a four-year apprenticeship perfecting classical French cooking skills. He met Peter Sullivan when they were both working at La Belle Helene on Sydney's North Shore. They then teamed up to open a string of successful restaurants: the Paddington Inn Bistro, Moran's and, most recently, the award-winning Aria Restaurant at Circular Quay.

Marinated and chargrilled leg of lamb with couscous and cucumber yoghurt

Guillaume Brahimi

Serves 6

1.8 kg boneless leg of lamb
100 ml honey
300 ml extra-virgin olive oil
2 tablespoons ground cumin
2 tablespoons coriander seeds
3 small red chillies, seeded and finely sliced
juice of 2 limes
1 clove garlic, finely chopped
1 Spanish onion, thinly sliced
2 cucumbers, thinly sliced
300 ml yoghurt
500 g couscous
salt and pepper
12 dried apricots, chopped
1 bunch coriander, chopped
1 bunch parsley, chopped
100 g almonds, thinly sliced

This recipe was cooked once a month by my mother, Yolande Brahimi, for a relaxed Sunday lunch with the entire family, who had to be present!

Lay the boned leg of lamb out flat. Massage both the cut and skin sides with the honey, olive oil, cumin, coriander seeds, chilli, lime juice and garlic. Leave to marinate in the fridge for 24 hours.

Gently mix the Spanish onion and cucumber into the yoghurt.

Place the couscous on a baking tray and pour 500 ml of boiling water over. Season with salt and pepper to taste.

Heat a barbecue or chargrill pan to medium and grill the lamb for 15 minutes on each side, or until done to your liking. Let the lamb rest for 10 minutes before slicing it.

While the meat is cooking, use a fork to break up the couscous. Add the apricots, herbs and almonds. To serve, place the couscous on plates, arrange sliced lamb on top and add a spoonful of the cucumber yoghurt.

Paris-born Guillaume Brahimi gained his Michelin three-star experience at La Tour d'Argent and Jamin in his home city. His success followed him to Sydney, where his restaurants Pond, Quay and Guillaume at Bennelong have garnered many accolades and awards. Guillaume at Bennelong, noted for its French-influenced modern Australian cuisine, was awarded *Australian Gourmet Traveller* Restaurant of the Year in 2003.

Kotlety with smashed sweet potato, spinach and beans

Teresa Cutter

Serves 6

2 onions, finely diced

⅓ cup chicken stock *or* water

500 g lean pork *or* chicken mince

2 cloves garlic, crushed

1 tablespoon freshly grated ginger

100 g shiitake mushrooms, finely chopped

1 carrot, finely grated

1 potato, peeled and finely grated

1 red capsicum, finely diced

2–3 teaspoons soy sauce

½ cup chopped fresh coriander

1 egg

1 teaspoon olive oil

Smashed sweet potato

800 g sweet potato

¼–½ cup low-fat coconut milk

ground ginger to taste

¼ teaspoon ground cinnamon

1 bunch spinach, leaves chopped and blanched

1 cup fresh soy beans
or 1 cup canned soy or adzuki beans, well drained

sea salt and pepper

My mother, Maryla Ostasiewicz, was Polish. She would make this dish about three times a week, along with *pierogi*, *bigos*, spag bol and braised oxtail. The recipe I give you here has undergone a little adaptation by yours truly, just to make it a bit healthier than the version Mum used to make. The rissoles (*kotlety*) are so soft and moreish that you'll make them again and again.

Preheat oven to 180°C.

Sauté onion until golden, using a little chicken stock or water instead of oil. Cool, then add to the pork mince along with the garlic, ginger, shiitake mushrooms, carrot, potato, capsicum, soy sauce and coriander. Mix well for a few minutes with your hands, then form into small patties the size of lightly flattened golfballs. (Make sure you squeeze out all the moisture from the potato before adding to the mince.) Heat the olive oil in a non-stick frying pan and cook the patties for a few minutes on each side, or until golden. Transfer to a baking dish and cover with foil. Bake for 45 minutes.

Meanwhile, peel the sweet potato, cut it into chunks and then steam until tender. Smash with the coconut milk, ginger and cinnamon until lovely and smooth. Fold in the spinach and soy beans, then season to taste with sea salt and pepper.

To serve, divide the sweet-potato mix between serving bowls and top with a few rissoles. Serve immediately and enjoy.

Teresa Cutter is one of Australia's leading authorities on healthy low-fat cooking. A qualified chef with fifteen years experience, she currently works as a freelance healthy-food writer for newspapers and magazines, appears regularly on TV and is a healthy-food consultant to doctors. Teresa has also published three cookbooks.

Hot and sour pork curry

Basil Daniell

This recipe for pork vindaloo was passed on to my mother by my grandmother. Pork is only eaten by Christian communities in Pakistan, as Muslims do not eat pig products. Good pork was difficult to purchase, and the pork suppliers usually only brought the meat to Christian households during special religious celebrations such as Easter and Christmas. It was therefore always a treat to eat this curry.

Note that you can substitute the pork with lean lamb or beef, if you prefer. And if a milder curry is required, use fewer chillies.

Serves 6

2 teaspoons cumin seeds

2–3 dried, hot red chillies

1 teaspoon black peppercorns

1 teaspoon cardamom seeds

3–4 sticks cinnamon

1¼ teaspoons black mustard seeds

½ teaspoon fenugreek seeds

5 tablespoons white-wine vinegar

1 teaspoon light-brown vinegar

1½–2 teaspoons sea salt

sugar

100 ml vegetable oil

175–200 g onions, sliced into fine rings

2.5 cm knob ginger, peeled and coarsely chopped

1 small head garlic, cloves separated, peeled and coarsely chopped

900 g lean, trimmed boneless pork shoulder, cut into 2.5 cm cubes

1 tablespoon ground coriander

½ teaspoon ground turmeric

Toss together the cumin seeds, chillies, peppercorns, cardamom seeds, cinnamon, mustard seeds and fenugreek seeds in a spice grinder (or mortar and pestle) and grind. Place the ground spices in a bowl. Add the vinegar, salt and sugar, mix and set aside.

Pour the oil into a wide, heavy-based frying pan and place over medium heat. Add the onion. Fry, stirring frequently, until brown and crisp. Remove onion with a slotted spoon and place in a blender. Set aside pan containing the onion-seasoned oil. Add 2–3 tablespoons of water to the blender and purée the onions. Add this purée to the ground spices in the bowl. (This is the vindaloo paste.)

Place the ginger and garlic in the blender. Add 2–3 tablespoons of water and blend until you have a smooth paste. Set aside.

Reheat the oil remaining in the pan over medium–high heat. When hot, toss in the pork cubes, a handful at a time, and brown them lightly on all sides. Remove each batch with a slotted spoon and set aside in a bowl. Reduce the heat to medium and add the ginger and garlic paste to the pan. Stir for a few seconds, taking care not to burn the paste. Add the ground coriander and turmeric. Stir for another few seconds, until fragrant. Return the meat and any juices to the pan, add the vindaloo paste and 1 cup of water, and stir to combine. Bring to the boil, then reduce heat to low. Cover and simmer for 1 hour, or until pork is tender. Stir a few times during cooking.

Serve with breads (parathas and chapattis), raitas (yoghurt dips) and pickles. If you like, this curry can be made the day before to allow flavours to develop.

Born in Pakistan, Basil Daniell is owner-manager of Sydney's innovative and acclaimed Oh Calcutta! restaurant, which is the only Indian restaurant in Sydney to have been awarded a prestigious chef's hat by the *Sydney Morning Herald Good Food Guide*. It won the Best Indian Restaurant category every year from 1995 to 2003.

Osso buco with borlotti beans

Stefano Manfredi

When I think of the food of my childhood in northern Italy, I can feel the seasons – each as clear and defined as black and white. In winter, the fog rising from the fields would distort the sounds of the world so that they seemed to come from another place. When I was six, I imagined this misty other world to be purgatory, the place between heaven and hell where, the nuns assured us, petty sinners spent time in penance for their misdemeanours. The fog was spoken of as though it were a plague, and the mention of it chilled us to the very bones.

When the fog was at its worst, my mother Franca and my grandmother would place large black cauldrons of minestrone on the fires and slowly cook osso buco so that the comforting and familiar aromas pervaded our home. Above all osso buco was, and still is, the food of my mother, and the comfort contained in this simple dish warms my bones and keeps the fog from seeping into my soul.

Serves 6

6 slices of osso buco (veal shank from the hind leg, cut across the bone), about 5 cm thick

1 cup plain flour

6 tablespoons extra-virgin olive oil

4 onions, peeled and cut into 2 cm chunks

salt and pepper

8 ripe Roma tomatoes, puréed

dry white wine

1 tablespoon plain flour, extra

2 cups freshly shelled borlotti beans

1 cup rougly chopped flat-leaf parsley

5 cloves garlic, crushed

Dust the osso buco on both sides with the flour. Heat half the olive oil in a frying pan and brown the meat lightly. In a lidded pot large enough to hold all the osso buco in one layer, lightly fry the onions in the remaining olive oil until transparent but not coloured. Arrange the osso buco on top of the onions, season a little with salt and pepper, and add the tomatoes and enough wine to just cover the meat. Bring to the boil, lower the heat to a simmer, cover and cook for 50 minutes.

Turn the osso buco, take half a cup of the liquid and mix with the tablespoon of flour. Return this mixture to the pot, add the borlotti beans, parsley and garlic, and simmer, covered, for another 30–45 minutes, or until the meat is tender. Season and serve with steaming polenta.

Stefano Manfredi is one of Sydney's most celebrated chefs. His eating establishments, The Restaurant (renamed The Restaurant Manfredi in 1993) and bel mondo, have received many awards including the coveted *Sydney Morning Herald Good Food Guide* three chef's hat award in 1994 and the Insegna del Ristorante from the Italian Government. Stefano also enjoys success as a food writer with his books *Fresh from Italy, bel mondo: beautiful world* and *Modern Italian Food*.

Braciolette napoletana

Armando Percuoco

I have strong, fond memories of my mother cooking this dish every Sunday in Naples when I was a child. I must admit that when I was older I used to beg her to cook something different, but now I am so happy whenever she serves up this dish. All those great memories come flooding back.

Braciolette Napoletana is a dish from the south of Italy. The ingredients combine two strands of our heritage: the ripe tomato is from southern Italy, and the pine nuts and raisins derive from the Arabs via Sicily.

Buon appetito!

Serves 6

1 large bunch flat-leaf parsley, chopped

50 g pine nuts

50 g raisins

2 tablespoons grated parmesan

2 eggs

2 cloves garlic, crushed

salt and black pepper

12 thin slices veal

1 large onion, chopped

½ cup olive oil

2 cups red wine

500 g ripe tomatoes, chopped

chopped flat-leaf parsley, to garnish

Mix together the parsley, pine nuts, raisins, parmesan, eggs, garlic, salt and pepper. Lay out veal, cover with plastic film and pound with a meat mallet until thin. Place about 1 tablespoon of the parsley filling in the middle of each slice of veal, roll up and secure with a toothpick.

Fry the onion in the oil until golden, add the veal rolls and cook for about 4 minutes over low heat. Add the red wine and allow to evaporate. Add the tomatoes and cook for 30 minutes.

Serve with a green salad and a good Italian bread.

Note: Leave the tomatoes in the sun for a day or two before using, if possible. Please do not use straight from the fridge.

Armando Percuoco was born in Naples. He worked for his father, Mario, at Le Arcate in Naples before the family emigrated to Australia in 1972. In 1979 Mario and his father opened Pulcinella in Sydney's Kings Cross, then in 1987 Armando opened Buon Ricordo in Paddington. It remains one of Australia's finest Italian restaurants.

Pot-roasted veal shanks with creamy mash

Wayne Rowe

Mothers seem to be the masters of slow cooking. I guess it has a lot to do with patience, nurturing and persistence. My mum, Phyllis Rowe, would start the day at the butcher's, where she would insist on frenched, trimmed veal hindshanks – one per person, and a couple for later on in the week with pasta – then move on to the local fruit and vegetable shop for potatoes, carrots, leeks, red onions and garlic.

This dish would take three to four hours to cook, slowly bubbling in the oven, and was served steaming hot with the mashed potato every mum makes the best.

Sear the veal shanks in a large pot over high heat. Season well with salt and pepper, add the onion, carrot, leek and celery and cook for 5 minutes, or until the vegetables are browned. Add the garlic, bay leaf, cinnamon, thyme and red wine, and continue cooking over high heat until the liquid is reduced by half. Add the tomato and stock, ensuring the veal is covered. Reduce heat to low, place a lid on the casserole and simmer for 4 hours.

When the meat is almost falling off the bone, remove the veal from the sauce, keep warm, season the sauce with salt and pepper and reduce for 10 minutes over gentle heat.

For the mash, boil the chopped potato in plenty of salted water until soft. Drain, return to the stovetop and continue cooking until all moisture has gone. Mash really well until smooth, slowly adding butter and cream and stirring with a wooden spoon. Season well.

To serve, place mash in large, shallow bowls, add one shank per serve, spoon over the sauce with all the vegetables, and garnish with parsley and lemon zest.

Wayne Rowe has worked at numerous restaurants of high repute in his eleven years as a chef, including the Savoy in London, the Regent Hotel in Sydney, and Peppers in Port Stephens and the Southern Highlands. He is currently executive chef at Sydney's Bambini Trust.

Serves 6

6 frenched and trimmed veal shanks

salt and black pepper

2 red onions, chopped

2 carrots, chopped

1 leek, chopped

½ stick celery, chopped

4 cloves garlic, chopped

1 bay leaf

½ cinnamon stick

1 sprig thyme

200 ml red wine

6 large tomatoes, deseeded and chopped

1 litre chicken stock

chopped fresh parsley, to garnish

grated lemon zest, to garnish

Creamy mashed potato
6 Desiree (or other waxy) potatoes, peeled and chopped

100 g butter

100 ml cream

salt and white pepper

Desserts,
cakes and
biscuits

Baked honey custards

Valli Little

I have fond memories of growing up in the United Kingdom in the fifties and sixties. There wasn't a lot of money around but we seemed to live well, supplied generously from Dad's wonderful vegetable garden. Special lunches and dinners would be timed to coincide with the arrival of new crops, like when the first Jersey royal potatoes were dug up. Mum, Iris May Hales, would cook a leg of spring lamb, and there would be fresh peas and home-made mint sauce . . . I can still taste it. Dessert would be something like these little custards – rich and quite delicious. Mum would serve them with a compote of whatever was in season. My favourite was blackcurrants, but rhubarb and cherries were pretty good too.

Serves 6

600 ml thickened cream

1 stick cinnamon

½ vanilla bean, split

5 egg yolks

1 egg

3 tablespoons honey

freshly grated nutmeg

Preheat oven to 140°C. Place 6 medium-sized ramekins in a baking dish.

Place the cream, cinnamon and vanilla bean in a saucepan and bring to the boil, then turn off the heat and allow to infuse for 5 minutes.

Place the egg yolks and egg in a bowl with the honey and whisk gently until combined. Add the hot cream, stirring to combine. Strain the mixture into a jug then fill each ramekin until almost full. Pour boiling water in the baking dish to come halfway up the sides of the ramekins, then carefully place the baking dish in the oven. Cook for 40–45 minutes, or until the custards are only just set. Remove from the oven and allow to cool until you can lift the ramekins from the water, then allow to cool to room temperature. (Try not to refrigerate these custards – they taste so much better when served at room temperature.)

Dust the custards lightly with nutmeg before serving them in their ramekins. Serve with a compote of seasonal fruits.

Born into a family of restaurateurs in the UK, Valli Little trained at the Cordon Bleu school in London. Since moving to Australia she has worked as a home economist and food writer, working on many successful titles including *Sydney Food* with Bill Granger and the Food of Italy and Food of France series. As Food Editor of the ABC magazine *delicious.*, Valli often produces more than 60 recipes each month, inspired continually by her travels and love of food.

Jeannine Dansereau's apple pie

Serge Dansereau

Mont St-Hilaire, near Montreal in Canada, is famous for its apples, but for me it was my grandmother's apple pie that was the true star of the town. The secret ingredient – champagne – gave the filling a magical sweetness, and the cinnamon, nutmeg and brown-sugar topping was nearly enough to ask for the pastry on its own. Grandma used to sell her apple pies at Grandpa's butcher shop, then she passed the recipe on to my mum, Jeannine, who shared it with me. My kids now love it just as much as I did.

Serves 10

Filling
100 g butter
1 kg green apples, peeled and diced
110 g sugar
125 ml champagne *or* sparkling wine

Pastry
125 g butter *or* margarine
55 g castor sugar
1 egg
260 g self-raising flour
35 g cornflour

Topping
1 egg yolk, beaten
equal parts cinnamon, brown sugar and freshly grated nutmeg

Preheat the oven to 180°C.

Melt the butter in a saucepan, add the apples and stir to combine. Add the sugar and champagne and cook until the apples are soft. Remove from the heat, allow to cool, then strain the apples of excess juice.

While the apples are cooling, make the pastry. Cream the butter and sugar together until light and fluffy, then add the egg and mix well. Sift the flour and cornflour together and stir into the butter mixture until combined. Wrap the pastry in plastic film and rest in the refrigerator for 1 hour.

Divide the pastry into 2 and roll out the first portion to line a flan tin (24 cm diameter). Fill the flan tin with the cold apple mixture. Roll out the remaining pastry and place on the top for the pie lid, joining to the base with a little water.

Glaze the pie lid with the beaten egg yolk. Combine the cinnamon, brown sugar and nutmeg and sprinkle evenly over the pie lid. Bake for approximately 30 minutes, or until the pastry is golden. Serve warm or cold, with ice-cream or cream.

Canadian-born Serge Dansereau began his career in Australia in 1983 at the Regent Hotel, Sydney, and after a year was appointed executive chef there. In 1989 he was voted Chef of the Year by the *Sydney Morning Herald Good Food Guide*. Serge now operates Bathers' Pavilion, at Sydney's Balmoral Beach, to great acclaim. He has recently published his third cookbook.

Effie's famous baklava

Bill Tikos

Among my fondest childhood memories is that of watching my mother, Effie Tikos, lovingly prepare the evening meal. I also recall the shared feeling of contentment as we finished every last delicious morsel on our plates.

Mum was well known for many Greek dishes by our extended family, who would gather together over Easter and Christmas. But her famous, rich baklava was the dish we all craved. Making baklava is a long process, but the results are very rewarding.

Serves 24

500 g chopped walnuts
2 tablespoons breadcrumbs
½ teaspoon ground cinnamon
½ pinch of freshly grated nutmeg
¼ teaspoon ground cloves
½ cup unsalted butter
185 ml vegetable oil
750 g Antoniou Fillo Pastry

Syrup
2 cups sugar
2 cups water
1 teaspoon lemon juice
1 stick cinnamon

Preheat oven to 200°C.

Place the walnuts, breadcrumbs, cinnamon, nutmeg and cloves in a bowl and stir to combine.

Melt 100 g of the butter in a small saucepan, add 150 ml of the vegetable oil and stir together. This mixture will be used to brush the fillo pastry sheets.

Lay out the first sheet of fillo and brush lightly with a little of the oil–butter mixture. Sprinkle 2–3 tablespoons of the walnut filling evenly over the sheet. Slowly roll out the sheet, enclosing the filling, and once you reach the end twist the roll into a coil. Repeat this process until you have used all the fillo. Brush the top of each coil with a little of the oil–butter mixture and then bake in the preheated oven for 30–40 minutes or until golden. Remove from oven and allow to cool completely in the tray.

For the syrup, combine all the ingredients in a saucepan, bring to the boil and cook for 15 minutes. Allow to cool a little, then pour the warm syrup over the cooled baklava until most of it has been absorbed.

Serve with coffee.

Originally from Melbourne, Bill Tikos founded the Sydney-based literary agency Diversity Management, which specialises in non-fiction including cookbooks. Bill's Greek parents instilled in him a passion for food and for cooking. Many of the family's meals were based on recipes handed down from his grandmother and great-grandmother, so food was also about keeping his cultural heritage alive.

Chocolate orange pudding

Geoff Lindsay

My mum Shirley's self-saucing chocolate pudding has remained a staple in my family's diet for as long as I can remember. It sustained me and my two brothers at least twice a week for twenty years. Two puddings, fifty-two weeks a year for twenty years . . . Is it possible that Mum has cooked it more than 2000 times?

Serves 4–6

60 g butter

zest and juice of 1 orange

1 cup sugar

1 egg

1½ cups self-raising flour

pinch of salt

2 tablespoons cocoa powder

½ cup milk

Preheat oven to 160°C.

Beat the butter with the orange zest. Add the egg and half the sugar, then add the flour, salt, half the cocoa powder and all the milk. Spread the mixture into a greased ovenproof dish.

Mix the orange juice with 1¼ cups of hot water and the remaining sugar and cocoa powder, and pour this syrup over the mixture in the baking dish. (If you prefer not to use orange juice, just add ¼ cup extra water to the recipe.) Bake for 35 minutes, or until the top is firm and the sauce underneath is thick.

Note: individual puddings are good for special occasions.

Geoff Lindsay is co-owner and chef of Pearl, one of Melbourne's most highly regarded restaurants. He has twice won awards for Best New Restaurant in Melbourne: Pearl won the award from the *Age Good Food Guide* in 2002; Stella, his previous restaurant, won a double award after it opened in 1994. Geoff was named Chef of the Year in the *Age Good Food Guide* 2005.

Pink champagne jelly

Alana Kennedy

When I was growing up my mum, Shirley Rose, kept an immaculate kitchen (and entire house, in fact). As well, she worked full-time and single-handedly brought up two daughters. Her recipes were quick and easy to make and clean up, and always delicious.

The same goes for this recipe, one of the oldest tricks in the book of treats, which I served on the occasion of my daughter's nineteenth birthday, when she invited her friends over for a *petite soirée* prelude to a night out on the town. My catering principles were: a little bit frivolous, tasty, very quick, not too fussy. Thus I decided on jelly – not frog-in-the-pond or a bowl of jelly, but a translucent, palest-pink jelly made simply with two bottles of pink bubbly, sugar and gelatine. Shimmery, gorgeous, girly. That evening, the jelly was entirely and very rapidly devoured and to my delight it became a legend, so I've been told. Since then, 'special occasions' cannot be mentioned in our house unless it's agreed that jelly *will be served*.

Serves 10–12

1.5 litres pink sparkling wine, at room temperature

1 cup sugar

30 g gelatine leaves

Heat 1½ cups of the sparkling wine in a small saucepan, then add the sugar and stir to dissolve.

Meanwhile, soak the gelatine leaves in cold water until soft. Drain and squeeze to remove excess water, then add to the hot wine mixture and stir over low heat until the gelatine is dissolved. Combine this warm liquid with the remaining sparkling wine and pour into a suitable-sized jelly mould. Place in the refrigerator to set (it is best to leave it overnight).

Unmould the jelly by dipping the mould quickly in and out of a bowl of hot water until the jelly begins to loosen from the sides. Carefully turn out onto a suitable platter and serve.

Alana Kennedy's background includes events management, catering, fine arts studies, illustration and design. She is currently engaged as a house manager in a private home in Melbourne, where she tends to the minutiae and the grandiose in the art of day-to-day living.

Claudia's tiramisu

Sally Gonano

My mother-in-law, Claudia Gonano, is a fantastic cook, the northern Italian food with which she grew up being her speciality. Once you've eaten Claudia's tiramisu you'll find that no other version compares. Hers is a traditional recipe in that it uses marsala, but she substitutes ricotta for the mascarpone. We only ever have this divine dish on special occasions, and I think it is best enjoyed this way.

Serves 10–12

4 tablespoons brown sugar

6 espresso-size cups hot Italian coffee

1 cup marsala

⅓ cup castor sugar

5 eggs, separated

1.5 kg ricotta

1 large packet savoyard biscuits

300 ml thickened cream

cocoa powder

extra cocoa powder *or* drinking chocolate *or* flaked chocolate, to garnish

fresh strawberries, to garnish

Dissolve the brown sugar into the coffee and add the marsala. Allow mixture to cool.

Meanwhile, add the castor sugar to the egg yolks and beat until smooth. Beat the egg whites until fluffy and add to the egg yolk mixture. Add the ricotta and cream, and beat until smooth and thick.

Dip the biscuits into the cooled coffee mixture and arrange in a tray or dish to fit snugly. (You can also make individual servings.) Spread a layer of the ricotta mixture over the biscuits, then sift a layer of cocoa powder over the ricotta. Continue to add layers of biscuits, ricotta mixture and cocoa until all the ingredients are used up. Finish with a layer of cocoa, drinking chocolate or flaked chocolate, and garnish with strawberries.

A Qantas flight attendant for many years, Sally Gonano married an Italian three years ago and was fortunate enough to inherit her mother-in-law's famous tiramisu recipe.

Trifle

Luke Mangan

Trifle was a huge favourite of mine as a kid, and I know where my mum, Marie Mangan, got her inspiration: *her* mum! I remember Nan making amazing trifles laced with sherry, port and wine. That's what makes this recipe, along with a sexy custard. When I think of trifles, I think of Mum and Nan.

Serves 6

Sponge
125 g sugar
4 eggs
100 g flour
25 g butter, melted

Crème pâtissière
2 cups milk
1 vanilla bean, split and seeds scraped
6 egg yolks
125 g sugar
2 tablespoons cornflour
icing sugar

Jelly
400 ml sugar syrup (make 1 litre from 500 g white sugar and 500 ml cold water, and store remainder)
3 gelatine leaves
½ punnet strawberries, hulled
1 punnet raspberries
1 punnet blueberries

To serve
100 ml strawberry liqueur
200 ml cream, whipped
grated dark chocolate

Preheat oven to 190°C. Grease 1 large or 2 small rectangular baking trays.

For the sponge, whisk the sugar and eggs together in a beater until doubled in size and light and fluffy. Sieve in the flour in batches, folding gradually through the mixture. When the flour has been incorporated, gently stir through the melted butter. Pour the mixture onto the greased trays and bake for 8–10 minutes, or until the sponge is golden brown and springy to the touch.

For the crème pâtissière, heat the milk in a saucepan with the vanilla bean and seeds. Bring close to the boil, then set aside for the vanilla to infuse. Whisk the eggs and sugar together until pale and ribbon-like, then sift cornflour in and mix thoroughly. Remove the vanilla bean from the milk and slowly whisk the milk into the egg mixture. Return mixture to the saucepan, place over low heat and stir until bubbling. Cook for 4 minutes, or until flour taste has gone. Transfer to a bowl, sprinkle with the icing sugar and refrigerate.

For the jelly, make the syrup by heating the sugar and water in a saucepan until the sugar dissolves (set aside the 400 ml you require, and store remainder in a sterilised jar in the fridge). Soak the gelatine leaves in cold water until soft. Drain and squeeze to remove excess water, then add to the hot sugar syrup, stirring to dissolve. Chill slightly. Halve the strawberries and scatter in a large casserole dish with the other berries. Pour the cooled gelatine mixture over the berries. Before the jelly sets, place a sheet of sponge over it and cut to size. Brush with the strawberry liqueur until soaked through. Refrigerate to set the jelly.

When ready to serve, mix the crème pâtissière with the whipped cream, spread on top of the sponge and sprinkle with grated chocolate. Or you can sandwich the sponge between two layers of the creamy custard and finish with extra berries.

Luke Mangan began his career under the tutelage of Herman Schneider at Melbourne's well-known Two Faces Restaurant, and then with Michael Roux in the United Kingdom. From there, Luke went on to open the acclaimed Salt Restaurant, Bistro Lulu and Moorish Restaurant, all in Sydney.

My mum's bread and fruit pudding

Alain Fabrègues

My mum, Carmen Fabrègues, was a talented hand in the kitchen, but she had some dishes she absolutely excelled at. This recipe is one of them. Bread and fruit pudding was a late-summer dessert made with the apples and pears from our small orchard. It also used cream from the fresh milk we would collect daily from the farm on the other side of the large paddock. As the milk wasn't pasteurised, Mum would boil it every evening, and in the morning she would collect the thick cream that had formed on the surface. She would then keep this cream refrigerated in a glass jar. When she had enough cream, along with a sufficient quantity of leftover bread, croissants or brioches, she could make her pudding. This is how the recipe goes.

Serves 12

150 g sultanas

50 ml rum

700 g bread, croissants, brioches *or* cakes

1 litre milk

1 vanilla bean, split and seeds scraped

3 apples, peeled and cut into 1 cm dice

3 pears, peeled and cut into 1 cm dice

100 g butter

250 g sugar

200 g cream

8 eggs

Preheat oven to 180°C. Butter a cake tin or baking dish and sprinkle with a few spoonfuls of sugar to coat the dish.

Place the sultanas in a small saucepan with 1 cup water, bring to the boil and cook for 2 minutes. Drain off the water, pour the rum over the sultanas and set aside, covered, for the sultanas to plump up with the liquor.

Cut the bread into pieces about 2 cm square and place on a flat tray. Heat the milk in a saucepan with the vanilla bean and seeds. Bring close to the boil, then set aside for a short while for the vanilla to infuse. Spoon the hot milk over the bread.

Sauté the apples and pears in the butter, adding a couple of spoonfuls of the sugar to lightly caramelise the fruit. Set aside.

Combine the remaining sugar with the cream and eggs, and pour over the bread. Place the sautéed apples and pears and the soaked sultanas on top, and gently fold in with a wooden spoon.

Empty the mixture onto the prepared baking dish and bake for 1 hour. Allow to cool and set for 15 minutes, then turn the pudding out onto a large plate. The sugar will have caramelised the edges, giving it a rich colour.

Serve hot or cold with custard or ice-cream.

The cooking of Frenchman Alain Fabrègues has been honoured in both his homeland and his adopted country, Australia. The Loose Box restaurant in Perth, of which he is owner and chef, has won many awards including *Australian Gourmet Traveller*'s Restaurant of the Year, and Alain has been declared Western Australian Chef of the Year five times. In 2004 he was awarded a French knighthood, at the rank of Chevalier, for his contribution to French culture and cuisine.

Lemon delicious

Stephanie Alexander

I have treasured memories of my mother, Mary Burchett, at work in our Aga-warmed kitchen and collecting produce from our garden. I learned to cook at her side.

This recipe comes from my book *The Cook's Companion*. It is a classic and in many families is the ultimate pudding – the golden sponge topping hiding a creamy lemon sauce. It can be quickly prepared and then slipped into the oven to cook as soon as the main course has come out.

Serves 8

2 lemons
60 g butter
1½ cups castor sugar
3 eggs, separated
3 tablespoons self-raising flour
1½ cups milk

Preheat oven to 180°C and butter a 1 litre ovenproof basin or serving dish. Zest 1 of the lemons and juice both. In a food processor, cream butter with the lemon zest and sugar, then add the egg yolks. Add flour and milk alternately to make a smooth batter. Scrape mixture from sides of processor bowl and blend in lemon juice. Transfer to a clean basin. Whisk egg whites until creamy and firm and fold gently into batter. Pour batter into prepared basin. Stand basin in a baking dish and pour in hot water to come halfway up sides of basin. Bake for 1 hour. Allow to cool a little before serving. I like it best with pouring cream.

Stephanie Alexander is arguably Australia's pre-eminent chef, food writer and educator. Stephanie's Restaurant in Melbourne set new standards in Australian dining for the twenty-one years of its life, 1976–97. She then opened Richmond Hill Cafe & Larder, a cafe and produce store which is also a popular venue for food events. Stephanie's acclaimed books include the phenomenally successful *The Cook's Companion* (now in a new edition) and, with Maggie Beer, *Tuscan Cookbook*.

Nanny Carrie's banana cake

Brett Glass

Nanny Carrie was always a good cook. In her early years, she used to win the cake contest at her local town fete in Bega. Now that I live in Sydney, my mum bakes the cake whenever I go to visit her. Thank goodness the cake gene got passed on to Mum, as this is a killer recipe.

Serves 10

125 g butter
1 cup sugar
2 eggs
3 ripe medium bananas, mashed
1 teaspoon bicarbonate of soda
½ cup milk
185 g self-raising flour
pinch of salt

Caramel toffee topping
2 cups brown sugar
½ cup milk
40 g butter
¼ teaspoon vanilla essence

Preheat oven to 180°C. Line the bottom of a 15 cm round cake tin with greaseproof or baking paper.

Place the butter and sugar in the bowl of an electric mixer and beat to a cream, then beat in the eggs, one at a time. Add the mashed bananas and keep beating. Add the bicarbonate of soda to the milk, then add this mixture to the batter. Beat well. Sift the flour and salt over the mixture and stir to combine.

Bake for 45 minutes, or until a skewer comes out clean when inserted into the centre of the cake. Remove from tin and cool on a wire rack.

For the caramel toffee topping, place all the topping ingredients except the vanilla in a saucepan and bring to the boil over medium heat, stirring until the sugar dissolves. Continue boiling for about 5 minutes until the mixture forms a soft ball when cooled in a glass of water – drop in a teaspoonful to test. Working quickly so the toffee doesn't set, spread the topping over the cooled cake.

Raised in the small country town of Bega in New South Wales, Brett Glass now resides in Sydney but regularly enjoys visits back home to relax and go fishing, surfing and take advantage of some great home-cooked meals.

Rhubarb daisy cake

Jamie Oliver

This cake was created by my mum, Sally Oliver, on the occasion of the birth of her second grand-daughter, Daisy Boo Oliver.

Serves 8

4 oz golden syrup

teeny bit stem ginger in syrup, finely chopped

grated zest of 2 lemons

vanilla seeds from 1 pod

750 g rhubarb (use nice, thin, pink stems, not bloody great tough old ends)

125 g butter

125 g vanilla sugar (made by adding vanilla seeds to castor sugar)

125 g self-raising flour

2 eggs

1–2 tablespoons milk (optional)

crème fraîche *or* fromage frais, mixed with orange zest, to serve

Preheat oven to 190°C.

Butter a high-sided, 30 cm cast-iron dish or non-stick frying pan. Add the golden syrup, ginger and ginger syrup, lemon zest and vanilla seeds. Now cut the rhubarb into 8 cm pieces. Take one-third of the slices and chop them into small pieces (these will form the centre of the daisy). I sprinkle about another tablespoon or two of sugar over the rhubarb before adding it to the mixture, or even a bit more golden syrup in the base. Arrange the rhubarb around the dish like the petals of a daisy, with the small pieces (on end) as the centre.

Mix the butter, sugar, flour and eggs together, and add milk if you want to (I think the cake is nicer without milk, but it can help make the mixture easier to spread.) Spoon the mixture over the rhubarb and level the top as best you can. It doesn't matter if there is some fruit showing through, although do try to get the topping as evenly distributed as possible.

Bake in preheated oven for 40 minutes, or until the cake is a lovely golden colour. Leave for 10 minutes in the pan before turning out. Serve warm with orange-flavoured crème fraîche or fromage frais.

British chef Jamie Oliver studied catering and then spent time in France before returning to London as head pastry chef at Antonio Carluccio's Neal Street Restaurant. Later working at the River Café, he featured in a TV program about the restaurant and was offered his own show. *The Naked Chef* was hugely successful. Jamie set up the Cheeky Chops charity, through which unemployed or homeless people are trained as chefs. He has written five cookbooks and fronted further TV series.

Love cake

Charmaine Solomon

Love cake is the traditional birthday cake in Sri Lanka, especially among the Dutch Burgher community. It is rich and spicy and probably derived its name from the fact that it was a labour of love – all those cashew nuts to chop by hand (those were the days before food processors liberated us from such tasks)! Every family had their own variation, and my mum, Kathleen Desmond (always called Kitty), liked to make it richer and moister than most. But basically the cake was the same as tradition dictated: very sweet, nutty and absolutely delicious.

Makes about 40 pieces

375 g coarse semolina

3 large eggs

2 large egg yolks

500 g castor sugar

zest of 1 lime, finely chopped

½ teaspoon ground cinnamon

½ teaspoon ground cloves

½ teaspoon ground cardamom

½ teaspoon freshly grated nutmeg

2 tablespoons rosewater *or*
¼ teaspoon rose essence

2 tablespoons brandy

2 tablespoons clear honey

½ cup evaporated milk

250 g raw cashews, finely chopped

1 tablespoon softened butter

Preheat oven to 120°C. Line a 23 cm square cake tin with two layers of brown paper and one of baking paper, allowing the paper to extend well above the height of the tin.

In a heavy-based frying pan, dry-roast the semolina over moderate heat, stirring constantly or shaking the pan, until the semolina is pale gold in colour. Turn out of the pan and leave to cool.

In the large bowl of an electric mixer, beat the eggs and egg yolks until frothy. Add castor sugar gradually, reserving 1 tablespoon. Continue beating until the mixture is thick and light. Add lime zest, spices, rosewater, brandy and honey and mix well. Gradually stir in the evaporated milk, then the cashews, butter and semolina, mixing thoroughly. Pour into the prepared cake tin and sprinkle with the reserved tablespoon of castor sugar.

Bake for 2–2½ hours. Cover the top with foil if the cake seems to be browning too quickly, resting the foil on the paper lining (make sure it does not touch the top of the cake or it will spoil the surface).

This is one cake you don't do the skewer test on, because if the skewer comes out clean the cake is over-cooked. It is supposed to be soft and deliciously gooey in the centre. Leave the cake in the tin to cool (it will take some hours). Cut into small squares to serve.

Love cake may be frozen in sealed freezer containers, and reconstitutes very well if left at room temperature until it is no longer chilled.

Charmaine Solomon has been the food editor of national magazines and has taught cooking on television, but it is for her thirty-one cookbooks that she is most well known. Her Asian cookbooks, in particular, have blazed a trail in the Western world, with the *Encyclopaedia of Asian Food* being nominated as one of the three best international cookbooks in the 1996 Julia Child Cookbook Awards in the United States, and winning the 1997 Silver Ladle Award in the World Food Media Awards.

Mum's Christmas cake

Nigel Slater

Mum treated cooking as just something that had to be done; she took no pleasure in it whatsoever. The strange thing is that every cake she baked tasted wonderful, as if baked by the angels themselves. Okay, they may have looked a bit wobbly (they usually sank, because she always opened the oven door too soon), but her Christmas cake was a particular joy for me. I know she wished she could have just bought one from a shop, but Christmas cake was my father's favourite thing in the whole world and she felt she couldn't let him down. Towards the end of her life, making the cake became a great trial, but still she did it, right up until the Christmas she died. This is the recipe I use to this day, and probably always will.

Serves 16

350 g butter

175 g light muscovado sugar

175 g dark muscovado sugar

5 large free-range eggs

100 g ground almonds

150 g shelled hazelnuts

1 kg total weight of dried fruits (prunes, apricots, figs, candied peel, glacé cherries), finely chopped

500 g mixed dried vine fruits (raisins, sultanas, currants)

5 tablespoons brandy

zest and juice of 1 orange

zest of 1 lemon

½ teaspoon baking powder

350 g plain flour

Preheat oven to 160°C. Select a 24 cm springform cake tin and line it with a double layer of lightly buttered baking paper, which should come at least 5 cm above the top of the tin.

Beat the butter and sugars in the bowl of an electric mixer until light and fluffy. Add the eggs one at a time (the mixture will curdle, but don't worry), then slowly mix in the ground almonds, hazelnuts, all the dried fruit, the brandy and the lemon and orange zest and juice. Now mix the baking powder and flour together and fold them lightly into the mixture.

Scrape the mixture into the prepared tin, smoothing the top gently, and place in the oven. Bake for 1 hour, then, without opening the oven door, reduce the heat to 150°C and continue cooking for 2 hours. Check to see whether the cake is done by inserting a skewer (a knitting needle will do) into the centre – it should come out with just a few crumbs attached but no trace of raw cake mixture. Take the cake out of the oven and leave to cool before removing it from the tin.

Born in Wolverhampton, England, Nigel Slater has worn the hats of cook, recipe tester and food editor, but it is as a food writer – and, more recently, television cookery-show presenter – that he is most well known. Nigel has been awarded Food Writer of the Year several times. He recently won a Glenfiddich Award for his autobiography, *Toast*.

Elsa's fairy cakes

Damien Pignolet

My mum, Elsa Pignolet, learnt to cook at her mother's side growing up in the Victorian country town of Rushworth. Elsa's delicious home cooking was served with a generous helping of love, and this is why I chose to spend my life cooking.

Her strength was in soup-making and our table was graced with wonderful broths and hearty offerings daily. Mum rarely made cakes but I remember a big plate of fairy cakes being served on my ninth birthday. Try this recipe and place a raspberry on each little cake for a real treat.

Fairy cakes
125 g soft butter
200 g castor sugar
2 large eggs
125 ml milk
1 teaspoon vanilla essence *or* the finely grated zest of 1 lemon
150 g self-raising flour
½ teaspoon baking powder
pinch of salt

Lemon icing
120 g soft butter
240 g icing sugar
1 tablespoon lemon juice
1 teaspoon finely grated lemon zest

Preheat oven to 200°C.

To make the cakes, place butter and sugar in a food processor and process for 1 minute until pale and light. Add 1 of the eggs and blend for 15 seconds, then repeat with the second egg. Add the milk and vanilla slowly with the motor running. Add the sieved flour, baking powder and salt, using the machine's pulsing action to combine the ingredients well but don't over-work the added mixture.

Line each compartment of a muffin tray with paper patty-pan cases and three-quarters fill them. Bake in the preheated oven for 5 minutes, then reduce the temperature to 180°C and bake for another 10 minutes or until golden. Remove cakes, in their paper cases, from the mould and allow to cool.

For the icing, whip the butter in a food processor until very light and then work in the icing sugar, processing until the mixture is pale and slightly fluffy. With the machine running, add the lemon juice and finally the grated lemon zest. Ice the fairy cakes when they have cooled.

Damien Pignolet is generally recognised as one of Australia's finest chefs and restaurateurs. As chef and co-owner of Sydney restaurants such as Claude's from 1981 to 1993 and Bistro Moncur since 1993, his eye for detail and his consummate French style have reaped many awards. He has also been an influential teacher of cookery for more than two decades. In 2004 he became executive chef and co-proprietor of the Bellevue Hotel Dining Room, also in Sydney.

Lozza's Anzac biscuits

Curtis Stone

My first-ever memory of good food was the fresh-out-of-the-oven smell of the Anzac biscuits my mum Lozza (Lorraine Coles) used to make. I used to watch her make them, and fight my brother to see who got to lick the wooden spoon. Now I live in the United Kingdom, Lozza still surprises me with a batch made in Australia and posted across the world.

Makes about 36

1 cup rolled oats

150 g plain flour, sifted

1 cup sugar

¾ cup desiccated coconut

125 g butter

1 tablespoon golden syrup

1½ teaspoons bicarbonate of soda

1 tablespoon boiling water

Preheat oven to 150°C. Grease 3 baking trays with butter.

Combine the oats, flour, sugar and coconut in a bowl. Place the butter and golden syrup in a small saucepan and stir over gentle heat until the butter has melted. Mix the bicarbonate of soda with the boiling water and add to the melted butter mixture. Stir butter mixture into dry ingredients.

Place dessertspoonfuls of the mixture onto the prepared baking trays, allowing room for the biscuits to spread. Bake for 20 minutes, or until lightly browned. Cool on trays.

Australian-born chef Curtis Stone began a degree in business before being lured into the kitchen, finishing his training at the Savoy Hotel in Melbourne. He went to London in the mid-1990s and worked for leading chef and restaurateur Marco Pierre White. Now consultant chef at Terence Conran's Bluebird Club, Curtis has appeared in a number of British TV cooking programs as well as the ABC's popular *Surfing the Menu* series (with fellow Aussie Ben O'Donoghue).

Ginger biscuit slice

Philip Johnson

The one recipe that springs to mind when I think of my mother Ruth's cooking is her famous ginger biscuit slice – 'famous', that is, because it was in the *Oxford Play Centre Cookery Book*. I grew up in Oxford, a small town in New Zealand, where all the mothers contributed recipes to be compiled into a book for fundraising. With a population of only about 1200, no-one dared submit a recipe that didn't work!

Makes 60 slices

250 g packet milk arrowroot biscuits
120 g unsalted butter, melted
⅓ cup condensed milk
¾ cup lightly packed brown sugar
60 g chopped walnuts
1 teaspoon ground ginger

Chocolate icing
90 g softened unsalted butter
90 g cream cheese
1¾ cups icing sugar
¼ cup cocoa, sifted

Grease a shallow lamington tin (or similar) approximately 20 cm × 30 cm.

Place the milk arrowroot biscuits in a plastic bag, lay on a flat surface and either roll over with a rolling pin or beat with a mallet to crush (not too finely).

In a large bowl, combine the melted butter, condensed milk, sugar, walnuts and ground ginger. Add the crushed biscuits and gently fold through. Spoon the mixture into the prepared tin and press in firmly using your fingertips. Smooth over with the back of a spoon (dipped in hot water if necessary). Refrigerate for several hours, or overnight.

To make the chocolate icing, place all icing ingredients in the bowl of an electric mixer and beat until smooth.

Spread a thin layer of the icing over the slice. Refrigerate until the icing has set.

To serve, cut slice into fingers approximately 5 cm × 2 cm.

New Zealand-born Philip Johnson has been cooking for twenty-five years, including a stint working in London with Anthony Worrall Thompson at dell'Ugo, and designing menus for Air New Zealand. He opened his Brisbane bistro, e'cco, in 1995 and in 1997 it was named *Australian Gourmet Traveller*'s Restaurant of the Year.

Acknowledgements

Firstly, thank you to all of the gracious and generous contributors who gave their time without hesitation, and to their wonderful mothers who shared their special recipes with us.

A huge thanks must go to the incredible Julie Gibbs, publisher at Penguin. What an extraordinary talent you are. Thank you for your unparalleled knowledge, humour and vision, and for having the courage to take risks.

To Sarah Dawson, my brilliant editor, thanks for your patience, commitment and enthusiasm for this project.

To the book's wonderful designer, Marina Messiha, photographer Mark Roper and food stylist Lisa La Barbera, special thanks for making the book look as delicious as the food.

Thanks also to the following suppliers of props for the photography: Aeria Country Floors; The Agent Group; The Essential Ingredient; Ikea; Simon Johnson; Marble Solutions; Market Imports; Railway Place Antiques; Step Back Antiques; Steptoe's Renovation Supplies

And last but not least, thank you to my mum Effie, whose passion for cooking gave me the idea for this book. Mum, your baklava is now finally immortalised, as it should be!

Bill Tikos

Index

Abacus beads (Chinese yam gnocchi) 65

Ajiaco (soup of leftover barbecued ribs) 27

Alexander, Stephanie 157

almonds

Rabbit with fresh almonds 100

apples

Jeannine Dansereau's apple pie 143

asparagus

Chilli prawn, asparagus and avocado cocktail 34

avocado

Chilli prawn, asparagus and avocado cocktail 34

Baked fish in paper 76

Baked ham 121

Baked honey custards 141

baklava, Effie's famous 144

banana cake, Nanny Carrie's 159

beans

Kotlety with smashed sweet potato, spinach and beans 128

Osso buco with borlotti beans 133

Bechamel sauce 58

Bedelis, John 10

beef

Chilli con carne 108

Meat pies 117

Meat rolls 56

Meat sauce 58

Moussaka 40

Polpettone al sugo (meat loaf in tomato sauce) 106

Ragu di Maria 56

Roast beef with Yorkshire pudding 102

Spaghetti bolognese 53

Steak and onion casserole 113

Wagyu beef and Guinness pie 105

Beer, Maggie 97

beetroot

Grandma Hewitson's borscht 24

Russian salad 32

Bennett, Shannon 105

Bilionis, George 39

biscuits and slices

Ginger biscuit slice 170

Lozza's Anzac biscuits 168

Blue grenadier with tomatoes 73

Boughenout, Meyjitte 7

Braciolette napoletana 134

Brahimi, Guillaume 126

Buttrose, Ita 91

cakes

Elsa's fairy cakes 167

Love cake 162

Mum's Christmas cake 165

Nanny Carrie's banana cake 159

Rhubarb daisy cake 160

Sponge cake 152

cakes, savoury

Steamed savoury pumpkin cake 13

Calombaris, George 68

Campbell, Joan 121

Cappelluti, Fernando 73

capsicums

Stuffed green capsicums and tomatoes 39

Caramel toffee topping 159

Carluccio, Antonio 106

casseroles

Mum's coq au vin 91

Oxtail stew 111

Pheasant casserole 95

Steak and onion casserole 113

Castellani, Robert 56

Cheese sauce 40

chicken

Chicken karage (deep-fried my mum's way) 89

Cock-a-leekie soup 21

Jenny Lee's roast chicken 92–4

Mum's coq au vin 91

Warm chicken soup 29

chicken livers

Chicken liver pâté 31

Preserved lemon and liver stuffing 97

Chilli con carne 108

Chilli prawn, asparagus and avocado cocktail 34

Chocolate icing 170

Chocolate orange pudding 146

Chong, Elizabeth 92–4

Claudia's tiramisu 151

Cock-a-leekie soup 21

Cocktail sauce 34

Codina, Javier 86

Coniglio al forno con prosciutto crudo e polenta (rabbit with Parma ham and polenta) 99

coriander

Orange and coriander roasted loin of lamb 123

Corn fritters with fried eggs and bacon 15

Cranston, Michele 29

Creamy mashed potato 136

Crème pâtissière 152

crêpes

    Sunday-morning crêpes 5

Crumbed fish 81

Cullen skink (smoked cod, salmon, scallop and potato soup) 19

curry

    Hot and sour pork curry 131

custard

    Baked honey custards 141

Cutter, Teresa 128

Daniell, Basil 131

Dansereau, Serge 143

Davie, Judy 21

Demasi, Laura 60–2

Dobson, Ross 113

Douros, Samantha Lee 58

Drennan, Matthew 83

duck

    Gnocchi con ragu all'anatra (gnocchi with duck ragu) 50

Dupleix, Jill 22

Durack, Terry 111

eel

    Jellied eel and smoked trout 32

Effie's famous baklava 144

eggplant

    Moussaka 40

eggs

    Corn fritters with fried eggs and bacon 15

    Flaky tuna and egg pie 83

    Potato and loukaniko scramble 42

    Stuffed eggs with horseradish 32

    Village eggs 10

Elsa's fairy cakes 167

Escabeche dressing 86

Evans, Peter 81

Ezard, Teage 108

Fabrègues, Alain 154

Fernandez, Angel 27

fish and seafood

    Baked fish in paper 76

    Blue grenadier with tomatoes 73

    Chilli prawn, asparagus and avocado cocktail 34

    Crumbed fish 81

    Cullen skink (smoked cod, salmon, scallop and potato soup) 19

    Fish cakes with tomato and herb butter sauce 75

    Flaky tuna and egg pie 83

    Jellied eel and smoked trout 32

    Linguini with blue swimmer crab, chilli, shallot and lemon 48

    Sardinas en escabeche (sardines in a traditional vinegar dressing) 86

    Stuffed squid 'in umido' served with polenta 84

    Tagliarini con sugo di calamari 55

    Whole steamed snapper with ginger and shallots 78

Flaky tuna and egg pie 83

Fulton, Margaret 45

Gilmore, Peter 114–16

Ginger biscuit slice 170

Glass, Brett 159

Gonano, Sally 151

goose

    Roasted goose with preserved lemon and liver stuffing, figs and caramelised garlic 97

Grandma Hewitson's borscht 24

Gravy 123

Grossi, Guy 55

Gusain, Hemant 37

Hafner, Dorinda C. 67

Halwa sabji (vegetable halva) 37

ham

    Baked ham 121

    Coniglio al forno con prosciutto crudo e polenta (rabbit with Parma ham and polenta) 99

    Split pea and ham soup 22

Hay, Donna 117

Herbert, David 76

Hewitson, Iain 24

honey

    Baked honey custards 141

horseradish

    Stuffed eggs with horseradish 32

Hoskin, Fiona 5

Hot and sour pork curry 131

icing

    Chocolate icing 170

    Lemon icing 167

Ingersoll, Jared 15

Jeannine Dansereau's apple pie 143

Jeffs, Janet 123

Jellied eel and smoked trout 32

jelly

    Jelly (berry) 152

    Pink champagne jelly 149

Jenny Lee's roast chicken 92–4

Johnson, Philip 170

Johnson, Simon 40

Jollof rice (West African pink risotto) 67

Kennedy, Alana 149

kibbeh

    Mishmisheeya (Syrian stuffed kibbeh) 118–20

Kotlety with smashed sweet potato, spinach and beans 128
Kurek, Iren 8
Kuruvita, Peter 48
Kwong, Kylie 78
Kyriakou, Theodore 100

lamb
    Lamb shanks with braised vegetables and mashed potato 125
    Marinated and chargrilled leg of lamb with couscous and cucumber yoghurt 126
    Mishmisheeya (Syrian stuffed kibbeh) 118–20
    Orange and coriander roasted loin of lamb 123
    Slow-braised cumin-crusted lamb shoulder with carrot purée 114–16
Last, Anna 31
Layered potato bake (rakott burgonya) 8
Lemon delicious 157
Lemon icing 167
Lemon oil 48
Linguini with blue swimmer crab, chilli, shallot and lemon 48
Lindsay, Geoff 146
Linguini with blue swimmer crab, chilli, shallot and lemon 48
Little, Valli 141
Locatelli, Giorgio 99
Love cake 162
Lozza's Anzac biscuits 168
Lui, Anthony 13

Malouf, Greg 118–20
Manfield, Christine 34
Manfredi, Stefano 133
Mangan, Luke 152

Marinated and chargrilled leg of lamb with couscous and cucumber yoghurt 126
Meat loaf in tomato sauce (polpettone al sugo) 106
Meat pies 117
Meat rolls 56
Mishmisheeya (Syrian stuffed kibbeh) 118
Moran, Matt 125
Moroccan salads 45
Moussaka 40
Mum's Christmas cake 165
Mum's coq au vin 91
My mum's bread and fruit pudding 154

Nanny Carrie's banana cake 159

O'Hare, Sarah 102
Oliver, Jamie 160
onions
    Steak and onion casserole 113
oranges
    Chocolate orange pudding 146
    Orange and coriander roasted loin of lamb 123
Osso buco with borlotti beans 133
Oxtail stew 111

Pang, Helen 65
pasta
    Abacus beads (Chinese yam gnocchi) 65
    Gnocchi con ragu all'anatra (gnocchi with duck ragu) 50
    Linguini with blue swimmer crab, chilli, shallot and lemon 48
    Pastitso (baked macaroni Greek-style) 58
    Quadretti e piselli (pasta with peas) 63

Rosa's lasagne 60–2
Spaghetti bolognese 53
Tagliarini con sugo di calamari 55
Pastitso (baked macaroni Greek-style) 58
pastry
    for apple pie 143
    Shortcrust 105
pâté
    Chicken liver pâté 31
peas
    Quadretti e piselli (pasta with peas) 63
Percuoco, Armando 134
Pheasant casserole 95
Pickford, Louise 95
pies, savoury
    Flaky tuna and egg pie 83
    Meat pies 117
    Wagyu beef and Guinness pie 105
pies, sweet
    Jeannine Dansereau's apple pie 143
Pignolet, Damien 167
Pink champagne jelly 149
polenta
    Coniglio al forno con prosciutto crudo e polenta (rabbit with Parma ham and polenta) 99
    Stuffed squid 'in umido' served with polenta 84
Polpettone al sugo (meat loaf in tomato sauce) 106
pork
    Hot and sour pork curry 131
    Rosa's lasagne 60–2
potatoes
    Creamy mashed potato 136
    Cullen skink (smoked cod, salmon, scallop and potato soup) 19
    Gnocchi con ragu all'anatra (gnocchi with duck ragu) 50

Lamb shanks with braised
vegetables and mashed potato
125
Potato and loukaniko scramble
42
Rakott burgonya (layered potato
bake) 8
Russian salad 32
Pot-roasted veal shanks with creamy
mash 136
Preserved lemon and liver stuffing 97
puddings
Chocolate orange pudding 146
Lemon delicious 157
My mum's bread and fruit pudding
154
pumpkin
Halwa sabji (vegetable halva) 37
Steamed savoury pumpkin cake
13

Quadretti e piselli (pasta with peas)
63

rabbit
Coniglio al forno con prosciutto
crudo e polenta (rabbit with
Parma ham and polenta) 99
Rabbit with fresh almonds 100
ragu
Gnocchi con ragu all'anatra
(gnocchi with duck ragu) 50
Ragu di Maria 56
Rakott burgonya (layered potato bake)
8
Rhodes, Gary 53
Rhubarb daisy cake 160
rice
Jollof rice (West African pink
risotto) 67
Riz au lait (sweet rice) 7
Simple gorgonzola risotto 68

Riz au lait (sweet rice) 7
Roast beef with Yorkshire pudding
102
Roasted goose with preserved
lemon and liver stuffing, figs and
caramelised garlic 97
Rosa's lasagne 60–2
Rowe, Wayne 136
Russian salad 32
Russian trio 32

salads
Chilli prawn, asparagus and
avocado cocktail 34
Moroccan salads 45
Russian salad 32
Shredded salad 45
Sardinas en escabeche (sardines
in a traditional vinegar dressing)
86
Sartori, Loretta 84
sauces
Bechamel sauce 58
Cheese sauce 40
Cocktail sauce 34
Meat sauce 58
Tomato sauce 60–2, 106
Tomato and herb butter sauce 75
Yoghurt sauce 120
see also ragu
sausages
Potato and loukaniko scramble
42
seafood
see fish and seafood
Shortcrust pastry 105
Simple gorgonzola risotto 68
Simpson, Darren 75
Slater, Nigel 165
Slow-braised cumin-crusted lamb
shoulder with carrot purée
114–16

Smoked cod, salmon, scallop and
potato soup (cullen skink) 19
Solomon, Charmaine 162
soups
Ajiaco (soup of leftover barbecued
ribs) 27
Cock-a-leekie soup 21
Cullen skink (smoked cod,
salmon, scallop and potato
soup) 19
Grandma Hewitson's borscht 24
Split pea and ham soup 22
Warm chicken soup 29
Spaghetti bolognese 53
spinach
Kotlety with smashed sweet potato,
spinach and beans 128
Split pea and ham soup 22
Sponge cake 152
Steak and onion casserole 113
Steamed savoury pumpkin cake 13
Stone, Curtis 168
Stuffed eggs with horseradish 32
Stuffed green capsicums and tomatoes
39
Stuffed squid 'in umido' served with
polenta 84
stuffing
for pheasant casserole 95
Preserved lemon and liver stuffing
97
for roast chicken 92–4
for roasted loin of lamb 123
Sunday-morning crêpes 5
sweet potato
Kotlety with smashed sweet potato,
spinach and beans 128
Sweet rice (riz au lait) 7
Syrian stuffed kibbeh (Mishmisheeya)
118–20

Tagliarini con sugo di calamari 55

Tasker, Alla Wolf 32
Terzini, Maurizio 63
Tetsuya Wakuda 89
Theodorou, Susie 42
Tikos, Bill 144
tiramisu, Claudia's 151
tomatoes
    Blue grenadier with tomatoes 73
    Stuffed green capsicums and
        tomatoes 39
    Tomato and herb butter sauce 75
    Tomato sauce 60–2, 106
Trifle 152

veal
    Braciolette napoletana 134
    Osso buco with borlotti beans
        133
    Pot-roasted veal shanks with
        creamy mash 136
Vegetable halva (halwa sabji) 37
Village eggs 10

Warm chicken soup 29
Wagyu beef and Guinness pie 105
West African pink risotto (jollof rice)
    67

Whole steamed snapper with ginger
    and shallots 78
Wood, Michael 19

yams
    Abacus beads (Chinese yam
        gnocchi) 65
yoghurt
    Cucumber yoghurt 126
    Yoghurt sauce 120
Yorkshire pudding 102

Zilli, Aldo 50

LANTERN

Published by the Penguin Group
Penguin Group (Australia)
250 Camberwell Road, Camberwell, Victoria 3124, Australia
(a division of Pearson Australia Group Pty Ltd)
Penguin Group (USA) Inc.
375 Hudson Street, New York, New York 10014, USA
Penguin Group (Canada)
10 Alcorn Avenue, Toronto, Ontario, Canada M4V 3B2
(a division of Pearson Penguin Canada Inc.)
Penguin Books Ltd
80 Strand, London WC2R 0RL, England
Penguin Ireland
25 St Stephen's Green, Dublin 2, Ireland
(a division of Penguin Books Ltd)
Penguin Books India Pvt Ltd
11 Community Centre, Panchsheel Park, New Delhi – 110 017, India
Penguin Group (NZ)
Cnr Airborne and Rosedale Roads, Albany, Auckland, New Zealand
(a division of Pearson New Zealand Ltd)
Penguin Books (South Africa) (Pty) Ltd
24 Sturdee Avenue, Rosebank, Johannesburg 2196, South Africa

Penguin Books Ltd, Registered Offices: 80 Strand, London, WC2R 0RL, England

First published by Penguin Group (Australia), a division of Pearson Australia Group Pty Ltd, 2005

3 5 7 9 10 8 6 4 2

Cover and text design by Marina Messiha © Penguin Group (Australia)
Photography by Mark Roper
Styling by Lisa La Barbera
Typeset in Bodoni by Post Pre-press Group, Brisbane, Queensland
Printed and bound through Imago Productions [F.E.] Pte Ltd, Hong Kong

National Library of Australia
Cataloguing-in-Publication data:

Tikos, Bill.
Mum's favourite recipes: classic home dishes from mothers
of leading chefs and other friends.

Includes index.
ISBN 1 920989 10 2.

1. Cookery. I. Title.

641.5

www.penguin.com.au

The pink ribbon logo is the registered trademark of the National Breast Cancer Foundation in Australia